Along the Indian

E. STANLEY JONES

THE ABINGDON PRESS

NEW YORK   CINCINNATI   CHICAGO

JONES
ALONG THE INDIAN ROAD

Copyright, 1939, by

E. STANLEY JONES

A1601089

CONTENTS

INTRODUCTION

THE Indian Road should have a peculiar interest to us at this period of the world's history. For on this Road a major discovery in human living has been made. The modern world has no widely recognized method between that of sitting down under disabilities, submitting to injustice and that of taking up of armed force to end those disabilities and injustices. It was submission or armed rebellion. It is true that constitutional methods through democracy came in to fill the gap. But there was a very great gap still open, for in many situations constitutional methods of redressing wrong were not available. A little man in India, dressed in a loin cloth, stepped into that gap with his method of non-violent non-cooperation. It was not necessary to sit down under disabilities, nor was it necessary to go through the brutalities of armed rebellion and war. A highly civilized, and to me a highly Christian, method was evolved and applied by Mahatma Gandhi when he said: "You need not sit down under wrong, nor need you go to war—refuse to cooperate with the wrong, take on yourself suffering, resist with weapons of infinite patience, go to jail en masse, match against physical weapons the weapons of soul force, conquer by a cross."

That, to my mind, is the greatest discovery made so far in the twentieth century. It opens up infinite possibilities.

A lad went into a bookstore in America and asked for a book entitled, *Jesus on the Warpath*. The clerk was puzzled until he discovered that he was inquiring for *The Christ of the Indian Road*. The only Indians the lad knew were the Red Indians, and the road they usually took was the warpath. So he pictured Jesus in war paint

7

on the warpath. I am afraid we of the older generation have done the equivalent of that. Only we have dressed Him in khaki and a steel helmet. Essentially it is the same—it is Jesus on the Warpath. But a new presentation of Christ has come. He is stripped of all these ill-becoming garments and is seen on the Indian Road more like He was on the Galilean Road. That new presentation of Christ has come through India and particularly through Mahatma Gandhi, a man not called by His name. Therefore the Indian Road must hold a peculiar fascination for us.

It is fourteen years now since I wrote the Christ of the Indian Road, and much has happened to India since then. This book is intended as a sequel to that first book.

The Indian Road is gathering up some of the intensities of the other roads of the world; life is being keyed up. But there is still a leisureliness about the Indian Road and conversation drifts from subject to subject as fancy suggests. This book partakes of that leisureliness. So I have been free to discuss many things as we journey along.

But do not think that because the Indian Road is leisurely, it is haphazard and goalless. On the contrary, there is a very serious vein running through the whole journey —it is all toward a Goal. And so it is with this book— we go into many bypaths, but the saving thing is that we know they are bypaths. At the close we come out at the Goal. The last word in this book is "Christ"—purposely so. For I try to make Him my last word on everything. "We always know where Stanley Jones is coming out," said Srinavasa Shastri, one of India's greatest Hindus, "for no matter if he begins at the binominal theory, he will come out at the place of conversion." Had he added, "conversion to Christ," he would have been more completely correct, for that is the center and goal of my life. It is the center and goal of this book.

A man was doing some repairs in the library of a friend of mine in America. He showed interest in the library and said to my friend: "You have a wonderful library. I wonder if you have a book here written by a man by the name of John Wesley; he lived out in India and wrote a book entitled *The Christ of the Indian Road*. He really was not as far off as he seemed to be, for the fact is that many men have had a good deal to do with the writing of my books, and not least of them, John Wesley. For I owe much to him and to many others as I journey along this Road. If every person I have met becomes a part of me, then many persons have helped me write this book. And since I meet most of all the Ashram group—for they journey with me—I owe them most. For we are in a conspiracy of love—a conspiracy to help each other even if the helping means preliminary hurting. Their minds and consciences trained through years of corporate thinking make a terrible gauntlet through which one must pass with a new book, and yet they can be very tender in their terribleness. Hence this book got through. I am grateful to them, and to my daughter Eunice, who has become my secretary. I have been used to secretaries in East and West who would mechanically take down what I say without comment. I could say what I pleased. But when your secretary is also your daughter, she feels she has liberties and duties and often looks up from the page with disapproving eyes and says, "I've heard you do better." It is disconcerting to say the least, but healthy. And when even she at the close of the journey said, "Well, if you cut out this and that, you'll have a really good book," I knew that it had passed the final test. It could go.

E. STANLEY JONES.

Sat Tal Ashram,
via Bhim Tal,
U. P., India.

CHAPTER I

THE INDIAN ROAD

THE Indian Road! The most fascinating Road of all the world. Every other Road seems tame alongside of this Road. There is no sameness here; and hence no tameness. A surprise awaits you at every turn. On this Road you will find the world's richest man and the world's poorest. You will find an age-long wisdom penetrating the masses along with one of the world's lowest literacy percentages. Along this Road you will find the world's most beautiful building—the Taj-Mahal—cheek by jowl with the world's most miserable hut. Here men disdain the world as evil and money as base, and yet on certain days will worship their own account books; and, when allowed, will enter the mints and fall down in worship before piles of bullion. Here you will find the gentlest souls of the world—that gentleness flowering into the Non-Violent Non-Cooperation Movement, a moral equivalent of war—alongside of which you will find an explosive mentality issuing periodically in the fiercest of communal riots—riots which would set India ablaze were they not put down.

On this Road you will be told that men are God and must be treated as such, and then you will find that a large portion of men are outcastes and are treated as such. Here you will find women set upon a pedestal and worshiped—is not India the Mother?—and yet alongside of it is the idea that "women and Shudras are born of the womb of sin," and a woman cannot be saved as a woman, but must first be reborn as a man to attain salvation. Here is the widest tolerance in religious beliefs alongside of the fiercest intolerance in social customs and caste rules. Here is a sense of Unity pervading all things and yet alongside

11

of it are the greatest gulfs that have ever separated man from man. Here the animal companions of the Road are held sacred, some of them worshiped, and then ill treated and neglected. Here is the world's most beautiful spirituality alongside of a materiality that has turned sacred places into systems of organized loot. Here the world and all it contains is Maya—illusion—and then it is fought over in courtrooms with a persistent tenacity that leads to the bankruptcy of everybody concerned. Here are the highest and most beautiful mountains of the world and the dullest of plains stretching in the shimmering heat. Here the peasant is the most docile and obedient of the world, and yet he is at this moment the world's most explosive material—a veritable tinder box, ready to burst into revolution, for he has nothing to lose except his debts. Here—but why go on endlessly from paradox to paradox? However, that endless paradox is India—fascinating, alluring, paradoxical India.

In the Khyber Pass, on the frontier of India, there is a road sign with a motor car painted on it pointing to one road and another sign with a camel and a donkey painted on it pointing to a road alongside—there the old and the new are kept separate. But that is on the frontier. In India proper the old and the new mingle in glorious confusion. The motor and the donkey dispute the right of way, the one with loud persistence and the other with silent patience. Whatever else the Indian Road is, it is never dull, for surprising paradoxes meet you at every turn.

It is no wonder that paradoxes greet you on the Indian Road, for into that Road has poured many a difference. The beginnings of this Road stretch far back into antiquity and its outlines are lost in the dim and misty past. Into this Road have poured the Turanians and the Aryans from the North, probably from Central Asia; the Sumerians from the West; the Dravidians from the South; followed by Moslem conquerors from the steppes of Asia. All these intermingling with the original inhabitants have formed in the process of time the Indian culture, basically and fundamentally Hindu, but greatly modified by the Moslem, and perhaps more profoundly by later Western contacts.

Into that culture have gone various and varying ideas about God and man and the structure of human society. Among the lesser ideas, four conceptions are distinctive and outstanding: (1) The Unity of all things, issuing sometimes in Pantheism, sometimes in Panentheism. (2) Karma, the law of cause and effect. (3) Transmigration, a corollary to Karma brought in to explain the inequalities of life; and (4) Caste. Society gradually hardened into a fourfold Varna-Ashrama, the caste system, literally "the color-system," based on the idea of the lighter Aryan being high caste and the darker inhabitants of the country taking their places as low castes and even outcastes. It seems that this "color-system" became at one time functional, dividing men according to occupation. But this no longer holds; occupation does not determine caste; birth does. Men on that Road were tolerant of the differences in ideas, but utterly intolerant of any breach in caste rules.

It is not difficult to recognize a Hindu upon that Road, but it is very difficult to define him. Various definitions have been given: "A Hindu is an inhabitant of India." "A Hindu is one who calls himself one." "Anyone in India is a Hindu who is not a non-Hindu." But the best definition I ever heard was given to me by a very able Hindu judge, who, when asked to define a Hindu, said, "Any good man is a Hindu—you're a Hindu." When I objected, and asked where the Hindu ended and the non-Hindu began, he added: "You can believe in anything and be a Hindu—anything from pantheism to atheism—anything, *provided you don't reject the rest."* There he put his finger on the genius of Hinduism—it is all-embracing. Believe anything provided you don't reject the rest! To the mind brought up in the atmosphere of scientific preciseness, to accept one thing is to reject its opposite. But not so in India. This statement of the Hindu judge is the key to India's history and to India's present. The genius of Hinduism is its all-inclusiveness. Nothing is rejected. Everything finds a place in its ample fold. In Conjeeveram is a series of temples beginning at one dedicated to cobra worship and going on through higher stages to one dedicated to the lofty philosophy of Ramanuja, who taught a philosophy of God closer to the Christian conception than any of the other Indian philosophies. A wall encloses both the temple of cobra worship and Ramanuja's philosophy and everything between. That enclosing wall is Hinduism. It is all-embracing. I was speaking in the sacred city of Benares when I was constantly interrupted by a pundit. After trying in vain to keep him quiet, he finally said, "Let me do one thing and then I will keep quiet." When I assented to his doing that one thing, he came forward and put some sandalwood paste on my forehead, the sign of an orthodox Hindu. "Now you are a Hindu," he said in triumph and then relapsed into quiet. Hinduism has put its mark on everything in sight—good, bad, or indifferent. That all-embracing attitude is its genius and its strength—and its weakness. It is its weakness, for life depends on elimination as well as upon assimilation. And Hinduism has lacked the power of elimination. Hence it is clogged.

But the greatest characteristic of the Hindu upon that Road—a characteristic that stands out among all others—is his God-consciousness, or, perhaps better, his God-hunger. Do you not see it in that faraway look in the eyes of the Hindu that seems to be looking beyond the material to the Unseen? The Westerner—and the Chinese—posit the material and infer the spiritual, the Hindu posits the spiritual and infers the material. He is sure of the one and not so sure of the other.

In the south of India there is a stone mountain, the great rock at the top forming an almost perfect human face—a face that looks up at the Sky with infinite wistfulness. That face is India. It has looked at the Sky with an infinite wistfulness through the long ages—India has hungered for God and still does so with an intensity unknown on earth.

When I arrived in Karachi after having come back to India through Russia and Persia, the very first sentence I heard from an Indian when I stepped on the shore was, "Whatever God says, that is right." How different from the Humanistic Road I had just trod in Russia! There the first word is, "Whatever scientific Man says, that is right." Of course India has had her skeptics too, but, on the whole, she journeys with her face at an angle— toward the Sky. Or perhaps it would be truer to say that India journeys with her eyes half closed, looking within to gain Self-realization, the God within. But whether she looks at the Sky for a transcendent God, or looks within for an immanent God, she is looking for God. Nelson once said, "The want of frigates will be found written upon my heart"—the desire for God will be found written upon the heart of India. If Kipling in his dying moment said, "I want my Heavenly Father," India in her living moments says, "I want to realize Brahma, to know that I am Brahma." "From the Unreal lead me to the Real," says the Upanishadic prayer, and to the Hindu that Real is God, the only Reality.

And yet, and yet, there are forces that are deeply at war with all this.

CHAPTER II

I STEP UPON THE INDIAN ROAD

At least three times I stepped upon the Indian Road before I arrived in India, once consciously and twice unconsciously.

The first time was when, as a student attending a Student Volunteer Convention at Nashville, Tennessee, I met for the first time an Indian. The impression lingers still—the soft white turban fastened so neatly; the flashing black eyes; the crisp but fluent English; the sense of being very ancient and very new; the breath of a spirituality which seemed not a veneer for an occasion but something from hidden depths; the gentle strength; the calm that came from the subconscious assurance that, having met many an emergency through a long racial history, he could meet many more and survive; the untapped resources that seemed to be hidden within him—all these things made me feel at once that I was in the presence of a person whose spirituality was an aroma, the breath of his very life, natural and unaffected. I remember nothing extraneous about him, except that he was a Brahmo Samajist, but the inner impression was very real —I was meeting the man whom I would meet again and again upon the Indian Road. He was to be my companion through life. Would he give me more than I gave to him? What *did* I have to teach a man like that? I felt very raw and undeveloped and rather abashed in the presence of this ancient something that looked out at me from his eyes. And I was to be a missionary to that "ancient something." Absurd! I would have turned back after putting my foot for the first time upon the Indian Road and renounced then and there being a missionary had I not felt that even amid my own rawness and lack of development I had something, Something, Someone whom I knew I needed and perhaps he needed too, being a man, albeit a very ancient one. Besides, when I really pondered over the matter, there was something about this spirituality that raised questions. Was it my own narrow prejudices, or was it a sure certain instinct that told me that this spirituality for all its pervasiveness and depth needed something, and needed it vitally if it were going to affect the world? Was it moralized? Was it socialized? These questions persisted, as I went away still enthralled by the astonishing impact of his spirituality. But even with those questionings, I knew in an undefined way that I had touched the man who might loose upon the world a spiritual power that might save it from its immersion in secularism and materialism. Had God saved this race for such an hour as this? And would God loose spiritual power upon this age through this race—a subject race—as He did through another subject race two thousand years ago? I thrilled at the idea, but I was also troubled by the persisting questions: Was this spirituality moralized? And was it socialized?

Thrilled and troubled, I put my feet consciously upon the Indian Road knowing that I was to adventure among a people who held the greatest possibility of being the source of a world spiritual renewal of any people on earth, but also knowing that if that were to take place, fundamental amendments would have to be made in that spirituality.

The second time I stepped upon the Indian road—this time unconsciously—was when listening as a youth to Dr. G. Campbell Morgan. A phrase he used haunted me for many years as I puzzled over its meaning. Why couldn't I dismiss that phrase from my mind as I had dismissed millions of other phrases? For twenty years it would come again and again with a haunting sense of life-significance in it. Then one day on the Indian Road its meaning dawned upon me and I saw that this phrase did have a determining effect upon my lifework and upon the Indian people among whom my life was thrown. The phrase was this: "A double-faced Somewhat." And the meaning seemed to be this: The God of the Vedantic philosophy was a Somewhat not a Someone, impersonal not personal. And in the best sense of that word, It was "Double-faced," in that in the Nirguna state It was without bonds or relationships or attributes, but in the Saguna state It was with bonds and relationships and attributes. It was, therefore, double-faced, for when It looked toward ultimate being, It was impersonal and unrelated and non-active; when It looked toward relative being, It was personal and related and active. Only in this Saguna state did It become incarnate or related to men in any way.

The Ultimate was double-faced. Only in its lower phase was It moral or serving or personal. In Its ultimate phase It was non-moral, lifted above moral distinctions. Further, It was lifted above all activity; It was non-serving. It was also lifted above personality—impersonality was the highest. Then morality and service and personality are not rooted in Ultimate Being? Do they belong only to a lower phase of life and will they be transcended as we rise to a realization of Brahma? Then morality and service and personality have no ultimate meaning? Will it not make a difference whether morality and service and personality are simply interim concepts and will be passed by when the goal is reached; or, whether they are rooted in the Divine, in His very nature, and therefore have permanent and lasting meaning? Would it not go to the very roots of life and influence the whole of life, individual and corporate, to hold one idea or the other?

That phrase haunted me intellectually for years—a

foretaste of the fact that it would actually haunt my life in India. The feeling of relativity in regard to morals and self-giving service and personality has been a persisting problem which has met me with its paralysis in actual life everywhere I turned.

The fact that personality, morality, and service are not rooted in the Ultimate has put its paralyzing hand on all three facts in actual life in India. They are not ultimately real—why bother to stress them now? We shall pass them by ultimately, why not now? Is this at the basis of the fact that reforms in India based upon emphasis on the worth of personality, of morality and service, flare up with tremendous enthusiasm and then sink back into ashes so quickly and so often? Does not the fact that they are not ultimately in God kill them in man? The ideas sufficient to sustain reform through thick and thin weaken at the Ultimate and hence let down the reforms.

No wonder "The Double-faced Somewhat" haunted me then, for It haunts me now as I meet It along the Indian Road.

The third time I put my feet upon the Indian Road was again in America, in my very first sermon. The little church was filled with my relatives and friends, all anxious that the young man should do well. I had prepared for three weeks, for I was to be God's lawyer and argue His case well. I started on rather a high key and after a half dozen sentences used a word I had never used before and I have never used since: Indifferentism. Whereupon a college girl smiled and put down her head. (I was very susceptible at that time of life as to what young ladies did or did not do!) Her smiling so upset me that when I came back to the thread of my discourse it was gone. My mind was an absolute blank. I stood there clutching for something to say. Finally I blurted out: "I am very sorry, but I have forgotten my sermon," and I started for my seat in shame and confusion. My ministry was starting as a dead failure. As a lawyer I had failed God. I had tripped up over "Indifferentism." As I was about to sit down, the Inner Voice said: "Haven't I done anything for you? If so, couldn't you tell that?" I responded to this suggestion and stepped down in front of the pulpit—I felt I didn't belong behind it—and said, "Friends, I see I can't preach, but you know what Christ has done for my life, how He has changed me, and though I cannot preach I shall be His witness the rest of my days." At the close a youth came up to me and said he wanted what I had found. It was a mystery to me then, and it is a mystery to me now that, amid my failure that night, he still saw something he wanted. As he and I knelt together he found it. It marked a profound change in his life, and today he is a pastor, and a daughter is a missionary in Africa. As God's lawyer I was a dead failure; as God's witness I was a success. That night marked a change in my conception of the work of the Christian minister—he is to be, not God's lawyer to argue well for God; but he is to be God's witness, to tell what Grace has done for an unworthy life. A lawyer argues from legalities and second-hand informations; a witness speaks of vitalities and first-hand transformations. Not that the whole case rested on what happened to me, but it did rest on what had happened through Christ—I was to be His witness, not my own.

I shall always be grateful for that failure—that bump shook a lot of false conceptions out of my immature soul. But why did that word "Indifferentism" trip me up? It seemed to me an ill-omened, sinister word, a kind of word that would haunt me through life. It has. When I used that word in my first sermon, my feet were unconsciously upon the Indian Road. That word would meet me again and again in life and as often would trip me up. It was my stumbling block as I began my ministry, and it has been the stumbling block of a great people through a long racial history. It is the chief stumbling block in India today as she faces reconstruction. Indifferentism stands as a huge solid boulder on the road of reform. If reform is to take place, it must go over or around or under this obstacle planted so firmly in the mind of India.

By Indifferentism I do not mean indifference; I mean indifference built up into a philosophical system and taken as a way of life, as a method of meeting life, or as the dictionary puts it, "systematic indifference, reasoned disregard." Life becomes hard and insoluble, so one steps off from it in disillusioned poise. He wraps his cloak about him and lets life go past, a vast panorama of illusion—he conquers it by a strategic retreat. That idea, in some form or another, is at the basis of almost all Indian philosophy. Moreover, it manifests itself in almost every religious attempt in India to find the solution to human living.

This has been the strength and weakness of Indian philosophy. Its strength, in that it has turned life in upon the inner spirit for the cultivation of inner states of mind. This produces the impression of spirituality when one meets a true Indian. You feel that he is concerned with states of mind rather than the state of things about him. It makes you feel that he is a spiritualized being. He is. It is easy to talk with the Indian about spiritual things. The Westerner is usually reserved at that point, not quite at home, and if he does talk about spiritual things, he appears hesitant and embarrassed. Not so the Indian. Spiritual ideas are on tap at once, and he talks about them fluently, easily, naturally. They are the breath of his life. And not only the breath of his life, but the strength of his life. It has given him resisting power against life all through the ages and has made him survive while other nations have gone down. The resilience of the Chinese and the retreatism of the Indian have made them survive as nations where other nations with more resisting, and hence more brittle, attitudes toward life have snapped and broken and perished.

It has not only helped the Indian to survive but it has produced an astonishing wealth of literature on the inner life. India has never written history—why should she? Life was but a panorama of illusion, not worth recording. The only reality was the *atma*—the spirit. Upon that subject she has produced in Sanskrit an astonishing wealth of literature, the discovery of which by the West has profoundly modified the thinking of the world. There are more words in Sanskrit describing the inner life than in any other language. The world is richer because of this emphasis thrown upon the inner life. It is India's strength.

But this attitude of Indifferentism has also proved India's weakness. It has helped India to survive up to a certain point—but only up to a certain point. A half-truth breaks down under the total pressure of life. Life finds its weakness. The weakness of Indifferentism is being manifest as the life of India is now being thrown open to pressures from every side. Demands are being laid on this philosophy of Indifferentism which it cannot meet—demands for reconstruction of the total life of India. Those demands call for positive thought and action, but Indifferentism is hesitant and retreats from life. Indifferentism would reduce the points of contact with life so that life would not hurt it on a wide front—you expect nothing from life, therefore it cannot hurt you. But these modern demands call for the opposite—they demand that you expose yourself to the needs of the underprivileged, the unequal distribution of wealth and opportunity; that the outer life be such that it will not be at war with the inner life; that the social, economic, and political order be recast on the basis of justice and brotherhood. This demands that the whole attitude of Indifferentism be reversed; that Sympathy ("suffering with") and Love ("sharing with") be the driving motives. In other words, there must be victory, but by an enlarging of life, a fuller life, so that you master outer life not by less life but by more life. One's spirituality must be positive not negative. It must win its battles in the midst of life by an offensive attitude resulting in the regeneration of the outer life, and not by a defensive attitude resulting in the degeneration of that outer life. There is no doubt whatever that while India has attended to her mystical states the outer corporate life has gone to pieces. The two have been compartmentalized—the inner unrelated, the outer unregenerated.

It is true that the poverty of India has had a great deal to do with this defeatism, but the underlying philosophy helped to produce the poverty. A vicious circle was set up. It is also true that foreign domination has contributed to Indifferentism. If the way is not open for national self-expression, the tendency is to drive one into a disillusioned attitude toward all outer life. But the underlying philosophy made possible the domination. Again a vicious circle.

When Jawahar Lal Nehru, one of the most honest and straightforward men in the world, said that the four great incubuses on the life of India today were "the Princes, the Capitalists, the Landholders, and the Sadhus," he was striking at this unrelated spirituality of retreatism which was no longer a drive but a drain. The problem would be comparatively simple were this Indifferentism only, or mainly, in the sadhus, for although they number six million, they could be eliminated. But the problem is larger. This attitude is all-pervasive in the minds of the laity except when it is being modified by other influences. It is tne rock upon which so many reforms go to pieces. They start out with enthusiasm, stimulated by some outward pressure, and then they slacken, sicken, and die—killed by the philosophy of Indifferentism. If reforms are being carried on—and, thank God, they are—then it is in spite of this drag of Indifferentism. But the casualties among reform movements are terribly heavy. The inner inertia wears them down. Tagore tells us that things come up to a certain point in India and then stop, dying of a certain poison. They do. The poison is the philosophy of Indifferentism.

The central problem of India is not untouchability, nor child marriage, nor poverty, nor even foreign subjugation—as great and insistent as these problems are—but the central problem is the inner philosophy of Indifferentism. Correct that and these other problems would fall as dead leaves before the rising sap of a new life.

But is not this philosophy of life rooted in a physical fact—the climate of India? Therefore, is it not ineradicable? Partly. There is no doubt that climate did pass over into an enervating philosophy of life and influenced it. But that should not make us hopeless about the future. Man, through modern inventions, is less and less dependent on climate. He is making his own. Besides, India, in the North, has six months of Paradise as well as six months of Purgatory. And then India is discovering her mountain resorts, and her leaders at least can conserve their energies out of the heat during the hottest months. After thirty-two years in India I find that if one has a hopeful philosophy of life, he can counteract outer climate by an inner one. I am stronger physically after these years in India than when I began. India also has the advantage of being able to live in the open air, a far more healthy habit of living than the closed houses of colder climates.

Remove Indifferentism and we can overcome climate. It is the mental climate that really matters.

Three things met me upon the Indian Road before I actually arrived in India: a double-faced Somewhat, Indifferentism, and a person with astonishing spiritual possibilities—these three things were the key facts to India's history, also the key facts of my own lifework among the Indian people. I was to try to loose this man's spirituality upon the world, but I should be blocked at every turn by two specters—a double-faced Somewhat and Indifferentism. I had two problems and a possibility.

CHAPTER III

MAKING PERSONAL ADJUSTMENTS

REALLY I did not intend to walk upon the Indian Road. As a student in college, I volunteered for Africa, under a presentation that made it seem as though one were signing his death warrant in volunteering. I am glad I volunteered under this grim presentation, for having consented to what I presumed would be death shortly after arrival on the field, I have looked on everything subsequently as sheer gain. I expected nothing from being a missionary except a quick passage to another world, so life since then has been one constant series of surprises. I expected nothing, so have not been disappointed. Someone has said, "In facing a problem, raise it in its most difficult form, answer it there, and you answer it all down the line." I raised the question of missions in its most difficult form— the very existence of the missionary himself—solved it there by an inner content, so that since then all the problems down the line have seemed less formidable.

Filled with a sense of missionary zeal, I felt that I should reverence any people to whom I should go as a missionary; so in the street car in a Southern city of America, I arose and gave a Negro woman my seat. The crowd tittered. I suppose I blushed, for I was very young and very sensitive. But as I look back now over a missionary experience of thirty-two years, I see that I had instinctively hit upon a most important attitude in the missionary, one without which one cannot succeed among my people. He must not come in pride of race and superior bearing—he must really respect the people to whom he goes. His message must be an offering, a love offering to the shrine of great possibilities.

26

I once saw an American traveler in India throw a beautiful California apple from the railway carriage window to the crowd standing on the station platform. He expected to see a mad scramble. But no one touched it; instead they stood around in lofty disdain and let the apple lie. He had thrown it! Had he called one to him and presented it as a friend—well, that would have been different. Much depends on how you present what you have to the East.

I never reached Africa, although an Indian youth in a Government college examination wrote in answer to a question about David Livingstone: "All England was upset over the disappearance of Livingstone in Africa and sent Stanley Jones to find him." I was late in arriving! I did not reach Africa until a year ago, but when I did arrive, I felt at once that I was among the people of my first love. I felt strangely at home. I suppose this must have shown in my manner, for an African teacher said to me one day in South Africa, "You're a white native." In my heart I have worn my new title proudly and have treasured it beyond the customary eulogies of chairmen of public meetings.

A white native! Every missionary must be the counterpart of that wherever he is. He can never look on "these people," and "this land" and "this Government"—they must become to him, "my people," "my land," and "my Government." In other words, he must become an adopted son of the land of his choice. It is not easy, however, to divest oneself of the consciousness of color, but some do get victory over it. "Thank God," said an Indian, "I have got rid of inferiority and superiority complexions." Glorious riddance! For why should there be superiority in color? "I am glad to introduce to you our colored brother," said an American chairman in introducing an Indian to an American audience, to which the Indian replied when he arose, "I am very glad to talk to you color-less people." It works both ways!

How happy I was to find on arrival in India that the people were colored! I cannot explain it, but I was distinctly elated at seeing the brown color. Was it because my first love was the dark African, and, in coming to India, I felt I was not deserting my colored people? Whatever it was, I have come to admire and love the soft-brown skin of the Indian. Other lighter shades seem colorless!

On my first trip to India on board ship, a British chaplain said to me in surprise: "What, you don't drink? You can't live in India unless you drink." To which I replied: "I don't have to live. I have another alternative: I can die. But some people have to live or they are in for it!" The grim basis on which I volunteered was holding me in good stead—it wasn't necessary to live, for I had consented to die. But concerning this matter of drink I felt then, and I feel now, that all taking of intoxicants is a failure of nerve, an escape mentality. One hasn't resources on the inside, so he tries to take them in from a bottle. It is crutches for lame ducks. After hearing me say that, a European one day went to the bartender and said, "Give me a crutch." He named it rightly! Men do not need "pick-me-ups" when they have resources within. In North India a banner was put up to welcome a General. On it were these words: "Welcome to the battle-scared General." The General was furious. They quickly changed it to: "Welcome to the bottle-scarred General." He could take his choice of banners! The fact is that those who are bottle-scarred are battle-scared—they try to dodge life by a subterfuge. When life gets hard and impossible, the West sometimes turns to liquor and sometimes to escapist religion; the East turns more consistently to escapist religion—in both cases a failure of nerve.

On that first trip out my cabin mate spent forty-five

pounds between London and Aden for drink. One night as I was kneeling beside my bunk for my good-night prayers, he tapped me on the shoulder and said, "Say one 'Hail Mary' and one 'Father' for me, won't you? Dick Kitchen is no man." He knew that he was trying to escape life instead of solving it—he was no man.

On that same first trip I overheard a young woman say to another: "I hear there is a young missionary on board. I hope he won't get hold of me." She too was trying to run away from life by being "fast." She was drugging herself with sex emotion so that she would not feel the disappointments and pains of life. Another case of failure of nerve. Before I arrived in India, I was meeting with this running away from life, an attitude I would meet all my days in the land of my adoption.

After all, there are just two ways to meet life: the one is to escape it, if possible; reduce life to that of the vegetable, pull in your contacts with life so that life will not hurt you, beat a strategic retreat, find the peace of submission. The other way is to get sufficient inner life to match outer life, conquer by the offensive, find the peace of victory. "I have come to get you out of life, and get you out quickly," is one remedy. "I have come that ye might have life, and have it more abundantly," is the other.

I distinctly remember my first impression of India as I came from Bombay to Lucknow—the inertia struck me like a blow. People were lying on beds in the daytime under trees, or they moved about very slowly. I was used to life keyed up and energetic. Here life seemed so run down and tired. Its poverty seemed to be accepted and life had adjusted itself to that fact. My first feeling was that in addition to my message about Christ I should try by my energy to arouse life and make it live. I took off the mudguards and the brakes from my newly bought bicycle. Why? I scarcely know, but I had the more or less unconscious feeling that in India the brakes were on life and I must take off my bicycle brakes as a symbol that I wanted India to take off the brakes. When someone asked me for the loan of my bicycle I told him it was "the one with the brakes off." Later in a meeting he told of my description of the bicycle and commented, "Stanley Jones is a man who physically and spiritually has the brakes off." Whether this was a good thing or not I do not know. I felt that something must arouse India and make her live. "You'll break down in a year at this pace," said a friend in caution. I did not break in a year, but at the end of eight and a half continuous years I did break. Before the actual break came, there was a very severe warning. Because of a run-down condition, chronic appendicitis became acute, and I was hustled from Sitapur into Lucknow in an Army truck at midnight to be operated on. Ten days later tetanus set in and it looked as though my missionary career were over. Bishop Warne, a saintly man, came to see me and get my last words. As he bent over me I whispered, "Please don't take away my work; I'll be well able to manage it." I had no intention of dying, and didn't! But when the war broke out in August, 1914, I was in the hospital with my open wound and nerves shattered by tetanus. The British surgeon was anxious to talk to me, a non-Britisher, about the war, little knowing how deeply he was upsetting me. I held the bed sheets over my lips so he could not see them quiver. Wounded men on a battlefield! I could feel every one of those wounds in my own wounded side. "Wounded" was not a word, but a fact. I winced under it all. But the world's wounds and mine have healed since that time, and now in our forgetfulness we have opened fresh wounds in the body of humanity. This time we may bleed to death. Humanity never thinks until it feels a pain, and the men at the top who guide nations into war seldom get wounded. They feel no pain, so they do not think. The men they send out to be cut to pieces are not wounded *men,* but "casualties." In the same way the economic wounds are not looked on as wounded men, but only as "the unemployed." Not so with Christ—when He talks of our wounds, He feels His own, hence the fellowship. No one has a right to speak to the wounds of the world except from his own.

I soon learned from my experience in India that I was wrong about trying to hustle the East by my own example of energy. I couldn't arouse India that way. I simply broke myself. The philosophy of India says: "If you are too energetic, life will hurt you—land you in a hospital. Slow down, retreat into inactivity and you will not suffer from activity." This is not a passing comment on life— it has been built up into a philosophy of life. Every system of philosophy coming out of real India, not influenced from the outside, ends up with Inactivity as the goal. The two great systems of real India are Vedantism and Buddhism. Of course there are the Bhakti and Karma systems, which point more toward positive action, but the two outstanding systems are these. In Vedantism Brahma is the actionless. Brahma is pure being without action in the ultimate Nirvana state. The highest man must be like the highest God, so he too becomes actionless; seated with attention concentrated between his eyebrows, he thinks himself into identification with the passionless, actionless Brahma. Buddhism is the same—Nirvana is literally the state of "the snuffed-out candle," so close to annihilation that scholars are still debating the question of whether it is annihilation or not. If it isn't the end of being, it is certainly the end of becoming. It is true that the Buddhist would counsel compassion and good deeds toward those who are bound up with the suffering of the world, and the Renounced One on his way to Nirvana should show compassion. But this activity is not in the goal itself, therefore it has no ultimate meaning. It is a passing phase. In like manner, the Vedantist modified by the Gita would counsel action, but action with no desire attached to it— *nish-kama karma,* "action without desire," for the desire brings one back into the wheel of existence. Even where there is action in the means it has no ultimate meaning, for it is to be passed by on the way to the goal.

I was entirely right in thinking that the idea of action as having ultimate meaning should be put into India's thinking, but I was entirely wrong in thinking I could do it by my own fierce activity. The Indian smiled at this fussy haste, it left him inwardly contemptuous, and as for oneself the end was a hospital with Mother Nature nursing her child back to poise and health. Besides, in this haste to get things done, one ran roughshod over tender susceptibilities and left hurt feelings behind. Twenty years later I had to stand up in a public meeting in Lucknow and ask pardon of an Indian Christian worker, a colleague who was associated with me in those hectic years. "I was more of a boss than a brother," I had to say to get the last stinging memory to the surface. Thus I had to straighten out the results of abortive attempts to hustle the East.

But this was not all. Physically I lacked poise, but mentally too I was not at rest. I came to India out of a very conservative training. There were no doubts because I had closed out all problems. I had a closed mind, closed upon the fact of the satisfying Christ within. If walls shut out other things, they also shut within one this precious Fact. But as the first disconcerting years of a missionary went by and my contacts with educated non-Christians became more intimate, my walls began to be assailed. They even crumbled before the revelation of such truth as this in the Hindu Scriptures: "You are to be like the sandalwood tree, which when smitten by the ax pours its perfume upon the ax that smites it." Was that not loving one's enemies and doing good to them that despitefully use one? But this came out of Hinduism. How could I relate my never-before-heard-of newness in Christ to this fact of evident truth and beauty found elsewhere? I studied the sacred books of other faiths, afraid of finding goodness and truth there. To find it would destroy my inward position. I had my back to the wall for several years. Only my experience of Christ held me steady amid the swirl of the mental conflict. Then one day I inwardly let go. I would follow where truth would lead me. I could feel myself turning pale as I did so. Where would it land me? I was letting go securities that had been satisfying for an uncharted sea. But after some time, when I looked back, I found that I came out not two inches away from where I went in. The great securities of my faith were intact. But now I held them because they held me. Intellectually I was free and unafraid. I was a follower of Christ with the consent of all my being. Christ was related to all other faiths as fulfillment. I saw Christ gathering up all these scattered truths within Himself and completing and perfecting them. I could therefore be the friend of truth found anywhere. Moreover, I could look with appreciation on the religion and culture of the people; I could be eager to see the best, for that best found fulfillment in Him. The newness in Him is not never-before-heard-of newness, but newness in the sense of completion, of perfection. It is a difference in degree, but the difference in degree becomes so great that it amounts to a difference in kind. However, it would be truer to say that other faiths are related to Him, not He to other faiths. He is the center from which everything derives its meaning, if it has any. "In Him all things hold together." If they are not in Him, they do not hold together—they go to pieces through inherent contradictions.

As John MacMurray says: "Christianity is true in the same sense that the force of gravity is true. If you think that you can jump over a three-hundred-foot cliff and not get the result in hurt, the answer is, you can't. If you think you can live on principles other than those embodied in Him, the answer is that you can't." Life simply won't approve of it. For He is Life. Something had come into life that became the Master Light of all my seeing. I knew that if I saw in His light, I saw; if not, I was blind. An objective standard of reference had come into life to which everything could be referred. "He has committed the judgment which determines life or death entirely to the Son" (John 5. 22, Moffatt). This is not a mere dogmatic claim of Scripture, but a proved fact of life. The whole of one's life begins to be one constant verification of this central truth in life. It puts a tingle into one's whole outlook, for one feels the thrill of being on the right track.

This new certainty was not something imposed, but something that grew out of the fact that life was one long verification of the central hypothesis of one's life. Wherever you looked and whatever you did and whatever you thought, you found that life worked this way and refused to work any other way. It was a certainty not founded on one specific fact, but on a lifetime of innumerable verifications that gather up into a stream that bears you along by its irresistible current.

"I am sorry to talk so much about Christ," said a brilliant Hindu lady, "but the fact is that I cannot help it." She naïvely expressed what is pressing on so many minds today—you may not follow Christ, you may not even love Him, you may even hate Him, but He is inescapable. Can the lungs escape air? the eye, light? the heart, love? the aesthetic nature, beauty? They can. But they cannot escape and live. If you want to live, you cannot escape

Life. And Christ is Life. Take any road you will in seeking Life and you end up at Him. Said a Hindu premier
of one of the provinces to me: "It is not a question of
opening the door to Christ—He comes in quietly and takes
possession." He does! And when He takes possession
of the mind, there is no further arguing. From that moment you *know!*

"I am afraid I have become one of those irritating persons who know that Christianity is true," said a professor
who had gone through doubt and skepticism to a living
faith. He was right, except that I would have changed the
word "Christianity" for "Christ." Christianity is not
true. It contains truths about the Truth. But it has a
mixture of error in it, for it is the system built up around
Christ and only more or less approximates His mind. But
Christ is the Truth. What each of us holds is truth about
the Truth, but in Him we have the incarnate Fact of
Truth.

I was sure of one place in my universe, one place that
I could utterly bank on—Christ. Let life do what it
would, how could it ever overthrow Life? "I cannot see
how you can stand to have a non-Christian chairman at
the close of your address break up everything you have
said by his remarks," said an earnest, but nervous de-
fender of the faith. My answer was simple: "If what I
have said can be so easily broken up, then it ought to be
broken up, for in that case what I said was only remarks
about life which can be broken up by further remarks.
But if Christ is Truth, then remarks about Him are like
the futile lapping of the waves around the base of Gibral-
tar."

Being sure of my Center, I could afford to be generous
in my outlook upon what others held. "He is a very
humble man," said a leading Hindu one day concerning a
certain Christian. "Yes," the other replied, "he is humble,

but deep down there is a sense of superiority. He feels that he has something of which he is so sure that he can afford to be humble." The Hindu was right. It is the centrally uncertain who are persecuting and intolerant. They objectify their inward fears. They are narrow because the basis of their inward certainty is narrow. They are bigoted because they are not big. The one who has found the central fundamental Rock doesn't get excited at every little approaching wave. The assurance of certainty is the secret of tolerance. I agree with Voltaire's definition of tolerance: "I disagree with everything you say, but I shall fight to the death for your right to say it."

How glad I was that those fierce, first days of lack of adjustment were over and my heart was at rest! In those early days I debated much with the non-Christians in public debates. But I soon saw the futility of it all. In a debate one doesn't want truth; he wants victory, and the barrenness of the victory soon becomes apparent. In those days we had an Indian Christian champion who was very formidable in debate with the non-Christians. He overwhelmed them with jawbreaking words and phrases. At the close of an attempt of an Arya Samajist to answer him, he arose in his two hundred-pound dignity and said, "If my opponent can even prove that he has understood my question, let alone answering it, I'll become an Arya." Much of the atmosphere of those days was dogmatism against dogmatism which quickly degenerated into a dog fight.

I got my feet up out of that entanglement of words against words and took my stand at the Word. Christ was my message. He did not come to bring a message from God—He was the message of God, not spelled out but lived out. This Word gathered up all lesser words within itself and fulfilled them. I was the friend of any truth found anywhere in India's faith, culture, and life.

I was at home and no longer a stranger in a strange land proclaiming a strange message. I knew that everything that went on before was for the sake of This.

But this attitude of appreciation of any goodness found in other faiths worked out into another direction. I began to appreciate Indian ability as well as the truths in Indian faiths. These two go hand in hand. Where one does not appreciate Indian culture and truths in her faiths, he usually disdains Indian ability. The relationship of the West with the East is strained, for it is founded on an overlordship, instead of a partnership. The white man goes on the assumption that this overlordship is natural, even God-ordained. It comes out in naïve forms sometimes. While on board ship to East Africa, an English lady, objecting to the Indian's claim to a fair share of the highlands of Kenya in Africa, said: "They have a country of their own. Why don't they stay in it?" It never occurred to her that she had a country of her own—why shouldn't she stay in it? She would probably have been shocked had some one suggested the counterpart of her statement. Similarly an Australian, in making an address defending the White Australia policy, said, "Some people quote the passage 'God hath made of one blood all nations that dwell upon the face of the earth,' but they also forget the rest of the passage: 'and hath fixed the bounds of their habitation.'" I quietly asked, "When did God fix the bounds? Before you got in or after?" The assumption is that it is always after! This position of overlordship is deeply challenged even though it often comes out in sullen resentment. An African teacher whose soul had been corroded by the acids of this assumption of superiority said to me: "There is one ray of hope for us. Europe is arming. She will blow herself and her existing institutions to pieces; then will come the colored man's chance." It was a bitter word, but who can blame them?

I sat in the Indian National Congress and heard several speakers refer to the coming world war as providing the chance for India's independence.

The overlordship must give way to partnership or there can be no peace either in the East or West. And this must be in the whole of life—political, social, economic, and religious. In Christian missions in India the relationships between East and West have not yet been righted. In China, for the most part, they have been righted. In 1927-28, during the anti-Western and anti-Christian movement that went across China, most of the missionaries were swept out. It looked as though years of effort had gone down in a crash and the Christian movement was doomed. But it was the best thing that ever happened to the Christian movement. In a few years the missionaries were again back, but back this time in a new position. The Chinese were now in charge of all educational institutions, and the missionaries were their helpers and stimulators and spiritual partners. The relationships between the Chinese and the foreign missionaries have been, in large measure, Christianized. The consequence is that Christianity has gone on by leaps and bounds since then. China is the ripest evangelistic field of the world today. The restrictions which were put upon Christian teaching in schools are now being taken off and freedom is being given. When I outlined the Christian program for reconstruction to a non-Christian Chinese governor, he replied: "It is a very good program. We will adopt it as our own as soon as the war is over." It took away my breath. But that is the spirit of China today regarding Christianity. One of the reasons is that Christian missionaries have entered into a partnership with China in which they are the servants of the situation and not its masters. And in losing their life they have found it again. Never has the missionary had such authority as he has in China today. It was the Chinese delegates who in the Madras Conference pleaded that more foreign missionaries be sent to China. And the appeal was sincere.

Perhaps one of the best things that could happen to Christian missions in India would be for the missionaries to step out for a period, say two years. In the meantime the heads of all institutions and other places of responsibility (including our Ashrams!) would be put in charge of Indians. Then the missionaries could return in a relationship of friends, stimulators, and helpers of an indigenous movement. They would become partners instead of overlords. If the fear is expressed that able men and women are not available to man the institutions and places of responsibility, the answer is that under present conditions it is a question if they will ever be available. For many of the best of the Indian Christians, seeing things closed at the top within Christian missions, go off into Government and other services, where everything is open. In this matter Christian missions are, in many cases, behind Government. There are exceptions to this, for in some missions everything is open—and more than open. Moreover, many Indians prefer service outside of missions because the financial emoluments are usually larger. But the general observation holds good.

As to efficiency, I am sure that Indians can, on the whole, be more efficient in their own environment and among their own people than can foreigners. The two brightest spots in the Christian movement in India are two places manned almost entirely by Indians. I refer to the Dornakal area with Bishop Azariah at its head and the Mar Thoma Syrian Church of Travancore. Both are going ahead by leaps and bounds. Bishop Azariah has gathered together over two hundred thousand converts in the last twenty years, and over a hundred thousand of those are in Bible classes every night of the year. Ninety per cent of them are in church every Sunday. The changed lives of these former outcastes are winning the higher castes to a Christian allegiance. Forty thousand of these high-caste people have already been won. Among the Mar Thoma Syrians of Travancore, India, a remarkable spiritual movement is taking place. This ancient Syrian church (called Syrian because their bishops were ordained by the Patriarch at Antioch) was probably founded by the apostle Thomas, but has been dead for centuries. But about seventy years ago one of their priests was converted. Thus began a Reformation. I often go to the great convention held yearly with up to forty-five thousand people in the audience. Only one thing draws them— a spiritual message, no sideshows, no drawing cards. Twenty-five thousand men on one side, twenty thousand women on the other, all dressed in white—intelligent, educated, cultured, spiritually susceptible. Tides of the Spirit go over these vast audiences and creative movements come out of this Spirit-impact. They begin a project on a shoestring and faith, and the faith wins out over the shoestring. For instance, they began a high-school building without enough money to pay a coolie to dig the foundation for the corner stone. "I lay this corner stone on air," said the bishop as he laid it. In three years five buildings were up and were crowded with students. Faith—initiative! The relationships between the sexes among the Christians of Travancore are the finest I know of any place in the world. Divorce and even unfaithfulness are practically unknown. In the West children arrange marriages and inform the parents; in Hindu and Moslem India the parents arrange them and inform the children. Among the Syrians, both parents and children are satisfied by mutual agreement, and then they go on. They have coeducation, and when I asked a headmaster if they

have ever had any trouble because of it, he replied,
"Yes, once we did have some trouble—a boy wrote a letter
to a girl." That was the sum total of his trouble from coeducation! In every possible way they are going ahead.

We need, therefore, not to be afraid of turning things
over to Indians. They will do it in an Indian environment
far better than we shall ever be able to do it.

But when the position of overlordship is changed for a
position of partnership, then the missionary will be needed
and welcomed for many years to come. He can bring to
the Christian movement in India the Christian heritage
of the West and thus cross-fertilize it. But in doing so
he will also take back to the West the heritage of India
and there will be a double movement. The most stimu-
lating thing that has ever come to Western Christianity
is its mission movement coming back to it in challenge and
a richer interpretation of its own gospel.

Moreover, the West must Christianize its relationships
with the Christian movement in India. The only Christian attitude is to be the servant of all. Anything less than
this or other than this is unchristian. And often our relationships are less or other than this. The fact that this
is so made an interpreter of mine change what I had said
in the following way: I had said that to be an evangelist
and also a Christian is very difficult—also to be a missionary and a Christian, or to be a bishop and a Christian is
difficult. The interpreter translated thus: "To be an
evangelist and a Christian is difficult, but to be a missionary or a bishop and a Christian is impossible." I wondered
if there was not something more than a slip of the tongue
in that statement! Unless the basis is that of being the
servant of all, the relationship is not Christian. On a
cathedral in Travancore a tablet says of a bishop, "He
ruled the diocese with great zeal and affection." He
ruled! It is true that we do not say that on tablets any

more, but we often do say it with our attitudes. This must cease if we are to be Christian.

Moreover, the East, when free to take from us, will do so in a way she cannot take now. Only when her soul is her own will she be free to accept from the outside. There can be exchange between equals, but between so-called inferior and so-called superior there can be no exchange, for the so-called inferior in taking gives his very soul. Once the Indian is on an equal footing he will take freely. I once said jokingly to an Indian nationalist who was wearing his little Gandhi cap and complaining of the heat, "What you need is a solar topi" (the pith helmet worn by the Westerner in India). He quickly replied, "The day we get Swaraj [self-government] I will have one." He couldn't take one under the circumstances— not until his soul was his own. India will never undertake reforms seriously until she is fully mistress in her own house. Now she is making a case for Swaraj, and to confess any need of reform is to give away that case. For instance, in one of the Legislative Councils a bill was introduced which provided for a certain needed social reform. One legislator said afterward that he agreed with the bill; the reform was needed, but he thought that the introducer was giving away their case for Swaraj, that what the mover said would be taken up by the enemies of Indian advance and be used against India. He therefore said that he had to take the other side in order to put something else on the records, for he knew those records would be scanned. We may not agree with this mentality, but we can certainly understand it.

One of the members of our Ashram, a strong nationalist, said in the course of a discussion that if the West has its aeroplanes, ancient India had her flying houses. "You don't really believe that, do you?" I inquired. "As an

Indian, I do," he replied. "As a man?" I asked, to which he quietly said, "As a man, I don't." The mentality is that India must prove herself as good as others, and if she finds difficulty in the present, she turns to the past.

It is true that with the coming of provincial self-government there is a greater freedom in the undertaking of reforms, but not until India is entirely self-governing will she be mentally free to confess a need of change. Now she is undertaking reforms haltingly and with apologies. Even so, tremendous reforms are taking place, but they will be sweeping only when India is sure of herself. You confess your need only when you are sufficiently sure of your position.

One of the reasons that India resents organized Christian missions as such is that she has the feeling that to be the subject of missions is to be in the category of "heathen" who are in special need. And there is no doubt that there is reason for her to resent this attitude of spiritual patronage, for many in the West hold it. I asked a clerk in Thomas Cook's office in London if I could get a missionary discount on a passage from Egypt to India, to which he replied, "No, for these discounts for missionaries are not from one heathen country to another, but only from a Christian country to a heathen country. For instance, we don't give discounts between Great Britain and America, for after all America is a so-called Christian country." Note the order: Christian, so-called Christian and heathen—these were the three categories in his mind! And he probably represents many. Until this attitude is wiped out, and we cease to see paganism as something on the map but as something in our own hearts in both East and West, and we see men as men in the same deep human need, apart from geography, this resentfulness will remain. And rightly so.

For instance, at the close of the address on the last

night of a series to non-Christians I usually say something like this: "I am going to allow those who want to go to leave, but I would like two classes to remain. First, those who are nominally Christians, but who haven't realized the Kingdom of God through a new birth; and, second, those non-Christians who feel themselves in the same need of finding the Kingdom through a new birth. I will not discuss the question of whether there is any other way to find the Kingdom except through Christ. I know this Way and I know no other. This Way works. I will not raise the question of baptism and the Christian Church here tonight. I believe in both, but that is something for you to decide as you study the Gospels and follow the light God gives to you. Tonight you face a previous question—the taking of the steps to find the Kingdom of God. I want to talk to you about those steps, and I want no one to stay who isn't prepared to take those steps for himself."

We then stand and have a silent prayer—I sometimes suggest that they pray the prayer, "Lord, what wilt Thou have me to do?" At the close of the prayer those who would like to go can retire and the rest sit down or come forward to the front seats. The response is usually very remarkable—say from one hundred to five hundred remaining. One of the reasons for this response is that the idea that the non-Christian is in special need is wiped out and the whole thing put on a human basis by asking the nominal Christians to remain also.

"How do you talk to Theosophists?" asked a Hindu one day, to which I replied, "I never talk to Theosophists, I talk to persons." We must talk to human beings, not Hindus; to men, not Moslems.

The human heart and the human mind are the same throughout the world, modified here and there by environment. A chief justice of Burma said to me, "I have been a judge in both England and Burma and I have watched lawyers in both East and West argue along the same lines and come out at the same fallacies. The human mind is one." This expert testimony was corroborated by another English judge who told me the same thing, namely, that all crimes are the same in East and West. He added that there were almost no criminals in India, only people who were aroused by a mob or sudden circumstance to precipitate action.

While in South Africa I asked the principal of Fort Hare College if the Indian students in the college were brighter intellectually than the Negro students, to which he replied: "They look brighter, but actually the examination results do not show them any brighter. Moreover, I have taught students in Europe, and these Negro students straight out of the Bush are as fine intellectual material as the students of Europe." That gives us hope for the human race.

It is upon this basis that I am a missionary. I find that when I go from country to country I do not have to recast my message. The approach may be different but the same human needs meet one everywhere. There are differences in development among races, but there are no permanently inferior or permanently superior races. If Christian missions had done no more than affirm and confirm that to the world, they were well worth while. For in this viewpoint there is hope for the world and hence hope for the peace of the world. There is no Eastern problem or Western problem—it is all melting into one human problem.

My position was clear. I could honestly say that in going to another people with my message I was inwardly free from snobberies and superiorities, for I knew that my own heart and my own people were in the same deep need of my own message as other people. Some time ago I was speaking in Ceylon and my audience gasped as I began repeating that famous missionary hymn which is so obnoxious to the Ceylonese:

"To Ceylon's isle,
Where every prospect pleases
And man is so worth while."

They gave a sigh of relief when I ended up that way. If Christian missions end up by saying that "only man is vile" when thinking of other races, then rightly those races are inwardly tight and resentful; but if we end up with the emphasis that "man is so worth while," then we are friends and helpers of the infinite possibilities in every man and every race.

We must confess, however, that we as Christians do retain one advantage—Christ and His Kingdom. We recognize how easy it is to pass over from the idea of a superior faith to the idea that those who hold it are superior persons, and we must be on our guard against this false assumption. Nevertheless, we cannot deny the central conviction of our lives. We repudiate all other superiorities—of class and race and color and learning, but at one place we do not budge—we believe that in Jesus Christ and His Kingdom we have found a spiritual Ultimate, and that this message is as necessary for every man as air is necessary to the lungs and love is necessary to the heart. As already suggested, the lungs can get along without air and the heart without love—but they cannot and live.

I had had to make many adjustments, but one place held steady.

CHAPTER IV

GETTING ADJUSTED TO REVOLUTION

THERE are parallels between what took place in Europe and what is taking place in India. Up to the Renaissance life was largely fixed and static, held in the grooves of the past. With the Renaissance, the rebirth of the mind, five revolutions were precipitated into the life of the West: the Intellectual Revolution, the Social Revolution, the Political Revolution, the Economic Revolution, and the Moral and Spiritual Revolution. These five revolutions were spread across five centuries, continuing on into the twentieth. In India these same five revolutions have been precipitated into the static, tradition-ridden life of "the unchanging East"—with this difference, that, instead of being spread across five centuries, as they were in the West, giving time to recuperate from one revolution to another, in India they were precipitated into this generation. It is true that India has been exposed to these revolutionary influences for a century and a half, but her power of resistance was so great that only now have these revolutions broken into the life of the masses in full force. Hitherto they had touched the educated fringe; now the center is giving way and revolution is in full swing. In no human unit, except China, has there been anything comparable to the spectacle of three hundred and fifty millions of people changing the very basis of their lives in five great departments of life.

In Russia after the Revolution took place some peasants wrote to Moscow asking for the photo of the new emperor, Revolutzia. In India Revolution is now the new ruler. The rule of this new monarch, which is displacing the rule of the agelong reign of King Dastur (custom), is creating betterment and chaos, hopes and fears, unity and division, light and shadow. In a procession moving along the streets of Calcutta there were two banners, one of which read, "Up with Revolution," and the other, "Down with Revolution." It was a slight mistake! But it really made no difference, for whether it was "up" or "down" it was revolution. The one cry heard in almost every procession and in almost every nationalist meeting is "Inquilab Zindabad!"—"Long live Revolution!"

It is not an easy thing to hand to the reader a photo of this new Emperor Revolution—it is so Janus-faced. Perhaps a few incidents here and there would give more insight into the appearance of this new ruler than a long, labored description. The Intellectual Revolution was precipitated when the mind of India began to turn from the past to the present and the future. That simple turning of the mind precipitated change in the total life of India. Mahatma Gandhi threw a bomb into the intellectual outlook of India when he said, "I will not accept the authority of Scripture when it is contrary to reason." There is enough dynamite in that statement to blow the foundations of religious authority to pieces. And that is what is happening. "Parmeshwar [God] is growing old and a new ruler is taking his place," said some villagers one day. Even the villager sensed the fact that the kind of God who demanded blind obedience is growing old and another kind of God is taking his place. The Intellectual Revolution is in full swing. In this Intellectual Revolution there is a frankness of mind being born which is making for intellectual realism. India has been the home of philosophy, but philosophy classes in the universities are being deserted for the sciences.

The second revolution, the Social Revolution, has been precipitated into the most static society of the world. The results are startling. Caste is going and going fast. But it is in all stages of dissolution. I sat beside a Brahmin at an international dinner. I could see that he was excited. When I asked him if this were the first time he had broken over, he replied that it was. "What will your family say about it?" I asked. He replied: "Well, I told them I was going to a tea party. They would not mind a tea party, but they would mind a full dinner like this!" Caste was giving way at the tea-party stage but holding the line at the full dinner—at the rice course in the dinner, to be exact. After I had had a meal with a group of Brahmins, I laughingly suggested, "Well, brothers, what happens to caste here tonight?" One of them replied: "You see, this isn't the proper way for a Brahmin to eat. He should be on the floor with a plantain leaf for a plate. Were we down there in the proper way, all caste rules would be in operation, but seated up here around the table all rules are suspended." A gentle transition! A Hindu was traveling with another Hindu in the train and invited him to partake of his food, which was refused. But he took tea and toast from the Moslem refreshment-room bearer, and when the other Hindu inquired how he could take food from a Moslem and refuse to take it from a Hindu, he replied, "Yes, but tea and toast are not mentioned in the Shastras [the Sacred Books], so they are allowed." Caste is in all stages of dissolution. But in some places it is still firmly in the saddle. Said a man in our Round Table Conference, "If by touching a glass out of which an untouchable had drunk I could get Swaraj for my country, still I would refuse to touch it." Caste is still firmly set in his soul. "For Dheds only" is a sign on compartments of trains going to the sacred city of Dwarka. The Dheds, a low caste, would defile, so they were segregated on this Hindu-owned railway. Many of the temples which under pressure were thrown open to the Untouchables were later "purified" and closed to them. But the worm is turning everywhere. The sign which was once in Shanghai, "Chinese and dogs not allowed," is duplicated on a temple in South India, "Europeans and dogs not allowed." In an Untouchable Conference a sign read, "Touchables and dogs not allowed." At a Nationalist Conference a sign read, "Government officials and dogs not allowed." And thus it goes, exclusion producing exclusion, but all the time caste becoming more and more untenable and impossible. In its dying throes it gives a kick in many a direction, but it is the kick of death, not life. It is still strong even in dying.

All sorts of explanations are given to uphold caste. I was in the train one day with a Brahmin, and when I asked him if he were going to have his meal in the compartment, he replied that he would have to have it in the Brahmin refreshment room. When I asked him if he were afraid of my evil eye, that it might pollute his food if I saw him eat, he replied, "They say that each person emits a different kind of electricity; that if a man who has a different kind of electricity from yours sees you eat, it stops digestion." This pseudo science has largely come from Theosophy, but it is impossible to bolster up a dying system. It is doomed.

Now, look at the revolution among women. I was once invited to speak in a palace of one of the rulers of India to the ladies of the palace. As I entered the large room, I wondered where my audience was, for no one was in sight, but I soon found they were there behind the screen across the center of the room. The only thing I could see of my audience was the bejeweled feet of these princely ladies. I talked to their lotus-feet! Compare that with another scene where, when I was answering a question about my views on Marxian Communism and was giving my objections, a little lady in front, with the vermilion mark of the orthodox Hindu upon her forehead, kept shaking her head in disagreement with everything I was saying. The shaking of that little lady's head is the shaking of a whole social system. Earthquakes that shake whole mountain ranges are feeble vibrations compared to the shaking of that woman's head. For that head had in it new ideas. And, as Goethe said, "There is nothing so powerful as an idea whose hour has struck." The hour of revolutionary ideas has struck. India is ready for change, and change there is in most unexpected places. Even the crowd behind the screen were not exempt, for one of those princesses was later killed while driving her own motor car. A daughter of one of those princesses sits beside me day by day at the table in this missionary home.

In Bombay there is a sign over a woman's club, "The world was made for women too." The ancient world which is going to pieces was not made for women—it was made by man for man, and woman fitted in where she could in this man-made world. But this new world into which India is going is being made not only for women, but by women. The greatest thing that has happened in India in the last ten years is the loosing of the power of womanhood into public affairs. Hitherto she has been the conservative power in India's life; now she is going ahead at breakneck speed. The power of womanhood is to be behind reform in the future. One man said to me: "I belong to two centuries. When I step into my home I am in the sixteenth, but when I step out I am in the twentieth, and I don't know to which I belong." But as we read some of the resolutions which are being passed by women's associations in India regarding birth control and kindred subjects, one wonders if this isn't the twenty-first century speaking!

I was speaking to an audience of Hindu women. A Hindu lady, the deputy president of the Madras Legislative Council, was in the chair. (By the way, in just what other country of the world is the deputy president of a Legislative Council a woman? And this is not a mere chance fact, for yesterday the deputy president of the Legislative Council of another province called on me to inquire about my health, for I had been ill—and she a Moslem lady!) In her chairman's remarks she said: "It is the men who have written our sacred books and it is the men who have degraded us in those books. I therefore suggest that we have no more men-priests, only women-priests." The women laughed and enjoyed my discomfiture—the only man "priest" there. But the gracious lady saved me from embarrassment by waving her hand and saying, "Oh, of course we would be willing to have men-priests after the manner of Stanley Jones." While this comforted me, I had no illusions about the meaning of it all. Here was revolution going to the very citadel, to the place where the Brahmin stood with an authority based on the fact that he was the mediator between Brahma and man. If that shook, then the whole structure of Brahminism went with it. And it is shaking. A Brahmin youth was riding a bicycle when his chain broke. He took off his sacred thread, which the Brahmin wears around his shoulders, and tied up the chain with this remark: "There, that sacred thread has been some use to me at last." In that playful remark can be heard the accents of a new world of thought.

The Minister for Self-Government of the United Provinces is a woman, Mrs. R. S. Pandit, one of the most gracious and charming ladies I have ever been privileged to meet. It might be noted in passing that the Chambers of the Legislative Council of the United Provinces used to meet in the palace of the last king of Oudh, a king who had one hundred and fifty wives in those very quarters. Now a woman is Minister for Self-Government in that very place! Ten new women's colleges have been opened in Lahore city alone in two years. Let that statement with its meaning soak in. For many years the Isabella Thoburn College, a mission institution, was the only woman's college in all Asia. Now ten new ones open in one city in two years! The social revolution goes on at breakneck speed, and yet it goes on with comparatively few casualties. Amid all the astounding changes taking place the woman of India is going through these changes with remarkable poise and balance, retaining that innate modesty and refinement and grace so characteristic of her through the centuries. She is sensibly keeping her sari, the most beautiful and graceful dress of the world. She is meeting these changes far more sensibly than many Western women who seem to be throwing away reserve after reserve of modesty until there will soon be nothing left. Perhaps the Indian woman, clad in her graceful sari, will be the figure, standing amid these wild extravagances, that will recall to other women what they have lost when they threw away modesty and delicacy. And perhaps one day she may save the situation to sanity.

Mrs. R. S. Pandit tells the story of seeing a man going along carrying an umbrella over himself and his wife behind carrying a baby and a bundle. "What's that?" inquired her twelve-year-old daughter. "That's India," replied Mrs. Pandit. To which the nine-year-old daughter indignantly replied, "Well, if I were in that woman's place, I'd walk ahead of him." "I wouldn't," said the twelve-year-old. "I'd walk alongside of him." Here we have three attitudes: behind the man, in front of the man, alongside of the man. Perhaps the pendulum will swing from the first to the second, but the rare sanity and poise of the Indian woman will bring it to the third—alongside of man, his gracious companion and helpmate.

I thought for a while that the wine of Western freedom

would go to the heads of the women of India and sweep them away from their wonderful poise and modesty. One such West-returned Indian girl, obviously tipsy, came up to me at a garden party and said: "I hear you have been in my city in the South preaching about some rot or other. So you're an American? How funny!" But it was not funny at all. I was brokenhearted. India's womanhood had come to this. But my load lifted when a few years later I heard she had changed. Her father undertook a fast unto death unless she gave it up. "Somebody had to suffer for me to redeem me," said this girl. I wonder if this capacity to suffer to help others will not hold those women steady who are about to be swept off their feet by modern life? I hope so. For the brightest spot in India's life is India's womanhood. Her poise, her modesty, her graciousness, her capacity to suffer make her one of the most attractive of the world.

They tell the story of a missionary lady in India who liked sheep's brains and ordered some. Her cook brought on the sheep's head without any brains in it. When the lady remonstrated about the absence of the brains, he quickly replied, "Madam, that is a female sheep—got no brains." It is a good story, but it belongs to yesterday and is told only by those who faintly hope for the good old days of man's supremacy. It is being knocked to pieces in a thousand examination halls throughout India. In the two mission colleges in my home city of Lucknow if the boys get more than fifty per cent marks in examinations, they feel they are doing very well, while if the girls get less than eighty-five per cent, they feel they are doing very badly. The examinations are the same. The man who said that "woman, being a rib from the side of Adam is therefore only a side issue," may have been a good punster, but he was a poor interpreter. Woman is no longer a side issue in India. She is at the center of every issue, increasingly so. The Social Revolution in India is in full swing.

The Political Revolution has been foremost in India because the most obvious. The die-hards shook their heads when the National Congress took over the Government in seven provinces under the Reform Scheme. They felt it was the beginning of the end of good government. India in her demand for self-government had said that "good government was no substitute for self-government," implying that they might not go together. But they have gone together. All the headshaking of the die-hards and all the misgivings of the nationalists themselves have been belied. Self-government has become good government, at least so far. I am not blind to the fact that a great deal of disillusionment has set in among Congress leaders as they see struggle for position and power take place in their idealistic movement. Nevertheless, the Congress group, with all their faults, represent the best character of India. They are men who have suffered for a cause. The Congress showed very great political astuteness in refusing to take office until the viceroy and the governors had committed themselves to a policy of practical non-interference with the elected ministers. It showed not only political astuteness but it showed too that congressmen were not overly eager to take office with all its emoluments and opportunities for the exercise of power. This was something new in political affairs—a hesitancy to take office! Moreover, it was something new when these elected ministers voluntarily cut their own salaries from four thousand rupees a month to five hundred rupees. This showed character, also insight, for India has the most highly paid officialdom of the world, all out of proportion to the economic life beneath.

This new Government is proving the thesis that we have always held, namely, that India would never really tackle the question of social reform until she was sure of herself politically. She is not as yet fully tackling the question, for she has only partial self-government, the Central Government is not yet in her hands. But she is introducing reforms that any alien government would hesitate to introduce. And were she not hampered at every turn by the Hindu-Moslem problem, a problem which still awaits solution, she would have gone much further. Amazing progress is being registered. This new nationalist Government has put in thirty-six hundred reading rooms and a thousand libraries in the villages of the United Provinces in less than a year. The Congress has shown a very great sense of responsibility and a very great capacity for government. And relations between Great Britain and India are better by far than for many a decade. Not that India has abated her demand for independence. But her energies are now being absorbed in self-government in the provinces, so that the demand for independence is not quite so vocal. Moreover, the fact of Japan looming on the horizon as a possible menace to the independence of India makes many thoughtful Indians hesitate about severing the British connection. An Indian High Court justice told me that during his visit to Japan they gave him their timetable: "Five years for the conquest and assimilation of North China, five years for that of South China, and in twenty-five years we will be able to take on India." This timetable is running ahead of schedule regarding China, so that India is getting really alarmed at the prospect. They prefer a receding democratic Britain to an advancing Fascist Japan. A very outstanding nationalist told me of his four "concerns": First, the relationships with Great Britain—we want complete self-government. Second, if we get that complete self-government, we are afraid of this new Fascist Japan. Third, the Hindu-Moslem relationships, the tension is growing worse. Fourth, the divisions and self-seeking within the Congress ranks itself.

The Indian really admires the British, though he fights them. In advertising a series of my addresses at the time of the non-cooperation movement, the local committee put down as chairman the first night, "Mr. Gupta, or substitute." The reason for "the substitute" was the fact that the Congress leaders were being picked off and sent to jail one by one, and the committee thought this chairman would be in jail by the time the meetings began. It was so. The next man in line to go to jail was the chairman that night and he arose and said, "We can thank our lucky stars that we are fighting the British and not some other nation, for the British have something on the inside of them to appeal to." Think of a warfare that allowed you to see good in your opponent! Those words confirmed within me the deep admiration I had for this kind of warfare that was willing to take suffering to gain its national ends, but was unwilling to inflict it. What moral and spiritual dignity there is in this kind of warfare compared with the barbarities of the other brand! It makes India seem to me one of the most civilized nations on earth when it was prepared to take the one and reject the other. Take this instance as a peep into the mentality of those non-violent non-cooperators: I was having tea with Doctor Ansari, a leading congressman, in his lovely home. I was reminded of the time when a British police superintendent came with a posse of police to search the house for anything seditious that might send Doctor Ansari to jail. While the search was going on, tea time came and Doctor Ansari invited the English police superintendent to have tea with him. And he did! What warfare! Mahatma Gandhi gave his watch to a policeman who was searching his belongings! When Easter day came, Rajendra Pershad, the present president of National Congress and "the Gandhi of Behar," wrote to the police superintendent saying that, since the next day was Easter and the superintendent might want to go to church, they would therefore suspend their civil disobedience campaign for that day and allow him to do so. What warfare! Those who take these weapons seem to me civilized men, and in comparison they make those of the military-frightfulness type look like savages straight out of the jungle brandishing their spears.

The Political Revolution in India by its very weapons has left a deposit of good will. It has done so both in the Indian and the British. The British were baffled by this new warfare. "If they would only fight with our weapons, we would show them a thing or two," said a sweating Englishman who had to deal with men who had an amazing capacity for passive resistance. But it was on another level, and the Englishman was not at home in this new warfare. "Let me carry your luggage for you," said a noncooperator to me at a railway station. And he did, although he was even then on his way to jail and in charge of the police. It is disconcerting, and, moreover, it is effective. It did not fail. The Non-cooperation Movement brought the Reforms. It compelled Englishmen to admire the Indian for whom he had had contempt. An English official went to see a non-cooperator in the hospital, a victim of a baton charge which the official was compelled to order. The non-cooperator with a cracked head said in greeting to the Englishman, "Well, I'll soon be well enough to go out and fight you again." Said the Englishman as he went away: "That is the most honest man in this town. I admire him." And one cannot help but admire the Englishman who called on him!

The European and the American with their ancestry of fighting men admire the man who fights back. They have a contempt for the non-resisting. This is the underlying reason for the American's different attitudes toward the Red Indian and the Negro. The Red Indian was a fighter; hence, there is no prejudice against him in America today; witness the fact that a full-blooded Red Indian became Vice-President of the United States and his Indian blood was never brought up against him. But one drop of Negro blood would have damned him. Why? One race fought us and the other allowed us to enslave them. The New Zealander respects the Maoris while the Australian has only contempt for the aboriginal. Why? One fought back and the other was mild and did not kill enough white people. This may be to the discredit of the fighting West, but it is a fact. Until the Non-cooperation Movement began the ordinary Westerner had a contempt for the Indians, except for a few of the martial races, but since the non-cooperation days the Englishman has been compelled to admire and respect men who had lost their fear of jail and baton charges. This fact has helped the Englishman to play the game in the Reforms, and even to stand at attention when the formerly hated national anthem of India is being sung in Legislative Councils.

To the credit of the Englishmen let it be said that they are playing the game in the new Reform Scheme even when they have to work under Indians who were formerly under them. An amusing instance of this is found in the fact that the chief secretary to the United Provinces Government, and in a way the private secretary to the premier, is an Englishman who hit the premier with a stick in a baton charge during the days when the premier was a noncooperator!

Another Congress minister transferred the Englishman who had been very severe on him during the noncooperation days and appointed the Englishman as secretary of his own department. A Congress premier presented the English chief secretary with a suit piece of khaddar (homespun) which the secretary wore to his office, although khaddar had been hated as seditious during non-cooperation days by most Britishers.

It is true that many British officials have never inwardly accepted the new regime and are counting the days when they can receive their pensions and get out of it all. But many are playing the game.

An Indian friend of mine was about to get into a first-class compartment of a train. An Englishman in possession objected. The Indian exclaimed: "You won't let me in? I'll punch your nose." To which the Englishman answered: "Oh, you're that kind are you? Come in and we'll talk it over." He did and they were soon friends! India has not punched Britain's nose, but she has shown that she can have her own head broken without wincing. She has shown no fear of jails and punishment, so the fighting West says: "You're that kind are you? Come in and we'll talk it over." The British official is now dealing with battle-scarred veterans of a non-violent war and he is playing the game with them, for in his heart of hearts he respects them.

This should teach us in the West that our Christianity will never be respected unless we can show a capacity to suffer for it, to die for it. If we had heads that had been broken, the people would respect the ideas in those broken heads. If we showed no fear of jails, we should have moral authority when we got out of them, or even while we lay rotting within them. Christianity conquered the fighting Roman by showing a capacity for being torn to pieces by lions without flinching. The Fijians believed that the man who had died a natural death was pursued by female demons as a coward—only the brave had any place in that spirit world. In this very material world of ours only the brave have a place, and Christianity will only have moral authority as it gets used to the sight of its own blood. The fighting races respect those who shed the blood of others; they will respect us when we show a capacity to shed our own blood in this non-violent positive resistance on the plane of active good will.

India's non-violent Political Revolution has been only partially successful because only partially applied, but that partial application has opened a door of hope out of war by showing how a dispossessed nation can gain its ends without recourse to the barbarisms of war. It is the greatest contribution that any nation has made to the collective life of the human race in the twentieth century so far. It has left a deposit in the soul of the race that will never die, and when we return to sanity from this present mad debauchery of armaments, we shall find that this is the one star of hope that has arisen in the darkness. It may guide us back to our Father's house from this far country. If so, India will be the saviour of the human race from self-destruction through war.

Among the five revolutions, the Political Revolution is dramatic and moving, but not nearly so consequential as the Economic Revolution. For this Revolution has more dynamite in it than even the Political Revolution. The Indian peasant has been the most docile and uncomplaining of any of the exploited classes of the world. For behind it all has been a philosophy—his present state is the result of Karma, deeds of a previous birth; if in this birth he is patient and obedient, he may get a better status in the next birth.

> The rich man in his palace,
>   The poor man at his gate.
> Karma made the high and lowly
>   And ordered their estate

would be the Indian version of a discarded Christian hymn. By the law of Karma everything that is is just.

All suffering is the result of antecedent sin. This has held sway for millenniums and has produced the most patient, the poorest and the most exploited peasantry of the world. If the Chinese have made of poverty a science, the Indian has made of it an art. The Indian is the most regal man amid his poverty of any man in the world. The poverty-stricken of the rest of the world are in rags and tatters, the Indian seldom. If he is not able to wear unpatched clothes, he wears none or very scanty ones. And he is usually clean where water is available. But while the Indian has a strong sense of bodily cleanliness, he has little sense of collective hygiene. The poor man in India talks of his wages in terms of half a stomach or a full stomach, and he means just that. Earning your daily bread means bread, not automobiles. Life is at that level for millions. A landowner told me he had seen his peasants picking out undigested grains from cow dung and washing them to eat them.

All of this has been accepted as sacrosanct. But in both East and West the eyes of men are being opened. We no longer sing the hymn ending,

> "God made the high and lowly
> And ordered their estate,"

because we do not believe it. We see very clearly how the so-called "high and lowly" arise, and we do not blame God, but ourselves. India's millions are beginning to realize that Karma too is not responsible. It is all man-made in this life and can be changed. That thought is the most revolutionary ever dropped into the mind of India. Of all the "dangerous thoughts" that is the most dangerous. And the Indian peasant is beginning to think it, and not only to think it but to express it. He is showing contempt for religion which would say to him,

"Stay in your sty,
Without a sigh,
And you'll get pie,
In the sky,
By and by
When you die."

His eyes are open. He is seeing causes and effects.

A banner in a procession of peasants in the Punjab read: "You drink your water after straining it, but you drink our blood without straining." You drink our blood! What a change from the title usually given to the rich, "Garib parwar" ("cherisher of the poor"). The mind of the peasant has swung into a new orbit, caught by a new idea, and the whole of life will have to readjust itself to that idea. Some would blame this consequent upset on a few agitators, but the real agitators are the unconquerable instincts of mankind which will not accept chains when they see they are chains, not garlands, hung around their neck by Karma.

A newspaper reported the great surprise of villagers when they saw camels and horses and oxen and sheep coming down into their villages from the sky in the form of balloons sent up by a Raja at a celebration at the birth of a son. They *were* surprised, and they will be more surprised to find out, as they are finding out, that those same horses and cattle from the sky were their own horses and cattle confiscated from them by bleeding taxation and rentals, now come back to their poverty-stricken villages as airy ghosts after first having amused the Raja. The Raja too will be surprised when the villagers connect the two. And they are connecting them.

A wealthy oil man traveling most of the time around the world bitterly complained to me of labor and its demands: "We will shut down our factories and our plants if they keep this up. And then what will they do?" he said with

finality, "for we can live without working—can they?"
No, they cannot. But he put his finger unwittingly on
the center of the economic problems of the world: under
this order some people can live without working *but most
people cannot.* That is the central injustice underlying
our present order. And this is the central adjustment that
will have to be made—"If a man will not work, neither
shall he eat." The Communists quote that sentence in
their Constitution, thinking they are quoting it from
Marx instead of from the New Testament! Wherever
it comes from it is right, for if we do not contribute, we
should not consume. The people in the Island of Samoa
call a childless wife "a food-waster," and one day we shall
call the non-workers the same.

The great city of Jerash, in Transjordania, was built
upon the incense trade. When the people were converted to Christianity, the incense trade founded upon
temple worship died and the city died with it. A city
perished by the simple changing of an idea. The present
world-order is founded upon certain ideas such as the
primary sacredness of position and property with only a
secondary sacredness of persons. Those ideas are changing and the order founded on them is perishing. It is
a time of heartbreaking change, but a new and juster order
promises to arise out of the ruins of the old.

No man in India is helping more to change the economic and social ideas of India than Pundit Jawahar Lal
Nehru. His very name shows the vast changes taking
place in India. He is a Pundit but has little or no use for
religion; he is a Kashmiri Brahmin, a Brahmin of Brahmins, but preaches equality of status and opportunity; he
is a scion of wealth, but he himself wears simple homespun cloth and desires a redistribution of wealth. He is
an honest, able and brave man, and India is tinder for
his teaching. He is putting the torch of his ideas into

this tinder, and soon India may be ablaze with economic revolution.

Pundit Jawahar Lal Nehru's amazing honesty is shown by the fact that, before he was elected president of the Indian National Congress the second time in succession, there appeared in the *Modern Review* an anonymous article dissecting his character, showing his quickness of temper and other weaknesses, and drawing the conclusion that he should not be elected. It was found out later, after his election, that he, himself, wrote the article!

I first met Jawahar Lal Nehru in one of my Round Table Conferences about fifteen years ago. When it came his turn to speak he said in his terse, staccato English: "I have dismissed God and religion from my life, for so many things are done in the name of God and religion which I cannot accept. I am trying to serve my country; if service to my country is religious, I'm religious, if it is not, then I'm not."

No wonder he has dismissed God and religion from his life when he sees how both were used to bolster up injustices and exploitation and die-hardism. If that were all there is of religion, we should join him in the dismissal, but, fortunately, that is not the whole story. God and religion have given birth to ideas and impulses that have produced the finest service to the race and will one day redeem the race. Did not even Professor Radha Krishna, the ablest exponent of the new Hinduism, say, "What does Christianity ultimately mean if it is not the power of love and suffering to remake society?" And Jawahar Lal, himself, spoke of "the rebel Jesus preaching non-violence and ahimsa and a revolt against the social order." He also sees distinctions in religion when he says, "The Sermon on the Mount and modern European and American Christianity—how amazingly dissimilar they are!" The fact is, that while he has apparently dismissed God and religion from his life, in reality he hasn't. "He often turns to the New Testament for comfort and strength in hours of discouragement," said his wife to a friend of mine. Besides, I wonder if there is not more real religion in his demand for social justice than in much religion that has no such demand. Jawahar Lal is like the son in the parable who said, "I go not, sir," and then went; and much of religion is like the son who said, "I go, sir," and went not. For there is more of God in justice toward man than there is in gestures before God without that justice. Many religious structures will have to come down that real religion may live.

But Jawahar Lal is wistful at times. This outburst bares his soul: "India is supposed to be a religious country above everything else, and Hindu and Moslem and Sikh and others take pride in their faiths and testify to their truth by breaking heads. The spectacle of what is called religion, or, at any rate, organized religion in India and elsewhere has filled me with horror, and I have frequently condemned it and wished to make a clean sweep of it. Almost always it stands for blind belief and reaction, dogma and bigotry, superstition and exploitation, and the preservation of vested interests, and yet I know well that there is something else in it, something which supplies a deep inner craving of human beings." "Something else in it"! There his wistfulness comes out.

I met Jawahar Lal again at a dinner party. When he was told that I was going to speak to students either in a near-by building, or they could bring the students into this large room and he could listen in, he eagerly suggested the latter. I really talked to Jawahar Lal that night, for I knew that he was the idol of students, even more than Mahatma Gandhi, and ideas planted in his great mind would come out on fire. For he is a brave and honest man.

I saw his bravery in one of the most touching incidents I
have ever seen. He was in jail at Almora and his charming and intelligent wife was ill with tuberculosis at
Bhowali Sanitorium, three miles from our Sat Tal Ashram. It was decided that she should go to Switzerland
and then to Germany for an operation upon the lung.
I asked her if her husband would go with her? Would
the Government allow it? I shall never forget her answer: "I do not want him to go with me unless he can
go as a free man." Here was a sick woman going to a
strange land to die, but refusing to have her husband
go with her unless he went on a basis her inward self-
respect could accept. I take off my hat. I did then. I
do again every time I think of it. And I keep my head
bowed in reverence as I see him spending twenty-four
hours with her before she left for Europe. The twenty-
four precious hours were up and the car that took her to
the plains went one way and the car that took him back
to his Almora jail went the other way. They could not
accept the Government offer of conditional release, that
he might accompany her. So they parted—for a principle. That is the stuff out of which this new India is
being made. Subsequently he was released, this time un-
conditionally, to go to the bedside of his wife to watch
her die. But the sight of the two cars going in opposite
directions will never be erased from my mind. Inwardly
I stood straighter, proud of being privileged to serve such
a people. They said my prayer at her bedside had helped
them.

At the dinner party mentioned above, as I spoke to the
students in the presence of Jawahar Lal, my host, Doctor
Higginbottom, asked him what he should reply to the
anxious cable of his daughter who had cabled from
America asking if there would be violent revolution in

India. "Tell her the Jumna won't burn," was his illuminating answer. The Jumna River won't burn, neither will non-violent India turn violent, was the meaning.

That was true, on the whole, in the political revolution. Will it remain true in the economic revolution? It will, if Jawahar Lal can control it, for, though he is a great admirer of Russia and what has happened in the Russian Revolution, he is also a disciple of Mahatma Gandhi at the place of non-violence. He would take the Russian Revolution without the Russian Revolution method. Barodin said to a missionary in China, "You Christians are trying to bring in the Kingdom of God by love, while we Communists are trying to bring it in by force." Jawahar Lal would side with the Christians in this matter, but he would not hesitate to use constitutional coercion through constitutional means. In other words, he would use the method of love, but love expressing itself as justice in human relations and using constitutional governmental means of enforcing that justice. And some of us as Christians would agree with him at that point.

Jawahar Lal disagrees with the Mahatma in many things and yet is fascinated by him. This sentence in a telegram to Mahatma Gandhi after his fast over the Communal Award throws light upon his attitude: "Am unable to judge from religious point of view. Danger your methods being exploited by others, but how can I presume to advise a magician. Love." Another passage from Jawahar Lal's *Autobiography* is illuminating: "Gandhiji did not encourage others to think; his insistence was only on purity and sacrifice. I felt I was drifting further away from him mentally, in spite of my strong emotional attachment to him. Often enough he was guided in his political activities by an unerring instinct. He had the flair for action, but was the way of faith the right way to train a nation? It might pay for a short while, but in the long run?"[1]

In regard to non-violence, he says, "The non-violent method, in order to justify itself, must be dynamic and capable of changing such a regime or social order. Whether it can do so or not I do not know. It can, I think, carry us a long way, but I doubt if it can take us to the final goal. In any event, some form of coercion seems to be inevitable, for people who hold power and privilege do not give them up till they are forced to do so. Conversion there must be on a large scale, for so long as large numbers are not converted there can be no real basis for a movement of social change. But coercion over some will follow."[2] Whether this means constitutional coercion of a minority by a majority or whether it is the coercion by a minority through seizure of power by military force is not quite clear. But my own view is that Jawahar Lal is such a disciple of Mahatma Gandhi that he would remain non-violent in a crisis. When asked whether he made non-violence a principle or a policy he replied, "Both."

The fact is that Jawahar Lal may do for the Economic Revolution what Mahatma Gandhi did for the Political Revolution, namely, he may make it non-violent. For he is really a disciple of Mahatma Gandhi at this point. If he does that, his achievement in the economic field will be as great as Mahatma Gandhi in the political field. It may be that through these two men two of the world's greatest contributions will be given. It is really one contribution, non-violent resistance, applied to two different realms, politics and economics. This would be the moral equivalent of war in both realms. A new door is thus

---

[1] Jawahar Lal Nehru, *Autobiography,* pp. 372, 373.
[2] *Ibid.,* p. 551.

opened to humanity out of the barbarities of international
and interclass war.

The economic front had to be taken over by Jawahar
Lal. Mahatma Gandhi is not capable of directing things
on this front. His mind belongs to another setting—it
does not grasp the essential factors here. At this place
the future belongs to Jawahar Lal and not to the Mahatma.
I saw the Mahatma sitting in his Ashram spinning his
charka on the banks of the Sabarmati River. On the
opposite bank the huge smokestacks of forty cotton mills
formed the skyline. The ascetic of Sabarmati turned out
by hand a few precious bits of yarn while these spinning
mills turned out tons. Mahatma Gandhi would win this
battle with the power age by sitting apart with his simple
charka; Jawahar Lal would move across the river and lay
siege to that whole citadel of power and capture it in behalf of the collective good and put behind those power
looms the social motive instead of the private-profit motive. Obviously, the future belongs to Jawahar Lal and
not to the Mahatma. Youth in India salutes the saint in
the Mahatma, but smiles at the spinner and turns to follow
Jawahar Lal.

I do not mean to say that Mahatma Gandhi has made
no contribution with his charka. He has. For the Indian
peasant with his small holdings is unemployed for about
six months of the year. Mahatma Gandhi put into these
spare hours this subsidiary occupation and thus filled a
very much-needed gap. But all this is only a temporary
expedient following the breakdown of the cottage industries by the coming of power machinery. Jawahar Lal
does not want merely to fill a gap; he wants to take the
center and make it contribute to the collective good. The
millowners are friendly to Mahatma Gandhi and contribute to his cause of political self-government, but they
are not so friendly to Jawahar Lal—they see where he is

driving. He has a program, and it means fundamental change.

He may be able to guide those changes through non-violent channels and he may not. For the landowners are arming for protection. In their recent meetings they have called on their fellow landlords to protect their rights by feudal armies of retainers. It is too late. The masses are awakening, the old docility is being sloughed off, rent collectors are being mobbed, the Revolution is on. The peasants are tinder for Jawahar Lal's teaching. One of the members of our Ashram making a survey of the economic condition of certain villages found every single man in certain villages in debt. So if revolution comes, they would welcome it, for they have nothing to lose except their debts. Some of the farseeing landowners see it and have accommodated themselves to ultimate defeat. "We are done for," said a thoughtful one among them to me. Others are hoping to postpone the inevitable. When I asked about the coming Economic Revolution, a Raja replied, "Yes, it is bound to come, our day is over, my only hope is that it won't come in my time." After me—the deluge! Others are trying to turn the tide. The British Government made the Communist party illegal in India and an Indian minister, Reddi, ordered all books on Socialism taken from the library of the Andhra University. Others simply try to deny its existence, but, as Phillips Brooks once said, "There are fifty ways to put out a fire, but denying its existence is not one of them." The fire is on!

This Economic Revolution is being led by a man who is sincere and able and determined, and very courageous. I listened to him in a National Congress speech and held my breath. He had just come out of jail—he would go back again if he kept up this kind of unvarnished talk! But the years in jail had not softened him; in fact, they had toughened the fiber of his spirit. What can you do with men for whom jail has lost its terrors? They will go far. And Jawahar Lal will go far, for high intelligence is linked with deep emotion and single-pointed sincerity.

His answer to my invitation to come to our Ashram at Sat Tal and lead our group on his favorite subject was illuminating: "I would really like to come, but I haven't the time." The Revolution was absorbing all his time and all of himself. Watch a man like that. He will go far. And remember that India is tinder for his torch. Watch the horizon for the blaze!

For Jawahar Lal has a growing mass of supporters. The growth of socialistic and communistic ideas in India is astonishing. I visited a few days ago the Vidyapith, an institution founded by congressmen during non-cooperation days, and found that the whole atmosphere was socialistic, if not communistic. It had been founded to promote nationalism, but was now promoting Socialism. A most significant change. About four years ago Mrs. Sarojini Naidu, poetess and nationalist, said to me, "Socialism in India is only in quotation marks." But now it is no longer in quotation marks, it is naturalized.

I found to my astonishment that there were six Socialist periodicals published in Lucknow. Almost all of them had sprung up in the last few years. No wonder a thoughtful man like Sir —, although a prince and a land-owner and far from being a Socialist, noted in his diary: "Within two years India will be Socialist." Some of the Socialists themselves are not so optimistic—they say twenty-five years.

Before we leave these first four revolutions, we must look at a special section of India called the Indian States and look at the revolution taking place there.

There are five hundred and sixty-two Indian States in India comprising one fourth of the territory of India.

They have direct relations with the Crown of Great Britain through the viceroy and are under Crown sovereignty, but they are independent in their territories. Their position is guaranteed by the Crown. In the old days when the rule became intolerable they were overthrown by the people, but this is now impossible, as the might of Britain guarantees the thrones of the Indian princes. Now and again Britain steps in and removes a too corrupt ruler, but, on the whole, the States are left intact.

One of the princes, on the eve of leaving his State after being deposed by the British government, ordered that bags of sugar might be dumped into the wells of the State so that the people's tongues being sweetened they might speak kindly of him after his departure. I need to drink of one of those wells, for it is not easy to speak kindly of the princes. These States are, for the most part, feudal. There are a few enlightened and progressive States, as Mysore and Baroda, where there is good government. The Gaekwar of Baroda, who has recently died, was a good ruler and a deeply religious man. While I was delivering a series of lectures in the Maharaja's theater to the public at Baroda, the Gaekwar sent word that he wanted to attend. Immediately all was excitement. The State authorities took over the theater, redecorated it, put up a throne in front of the platform with a silver chair on it. An invitation to the officials was given by the Gaekwar, and an invitation from a ruler is a command, so they were all there from the prime minister down. It was literally witnessing before kings and governors. He held my hand a long time in both of his at the close and said, "I'm trying to live what you have been talking about." I think he was.

On another visit the Gaekwar invited me to speak in the beautiful palace hall, the most beautiful hall I have ever spoken in. Again all the officials were there and the

British Resident also. The students clamored to get in, but were not allowed, as the hall was filled. They demanded that they be allowed to sit on the marble floors. They made such a clamor that they were finally allowed. I did not trim my message to that assembly—it was straightforwardly Christian.

I had word that the Gaekwar had approved the granting of a thousand rupees for the printing of the address. But, like many things, it must have been held up on the way—I never received it!

Once a famous sannyasi was lecturing before the Gaekwar on Hindu philosophy, and when the time came for him to stop he was going strong. The Gaekwar held up his hand as a signal to stop and then asked him this question, "Now, tell me, what has all this to do with my personal life?" The sannyasi, nonplussed, grinned a helpless grin and said nothing. "I thought so," said the Gaekwar, as he walked away. It had nothing to do with life. He wanted something to help him to be a better man and a better ruler.

When he heard about the Laubach method of abolishing adult illiteracy, which I was advocating, he sent for me to demonstrate it before his officials. The essence of the method is that the adult illiterate can be taught to read in about thirteen lessons. When given his first lesson, he is told that he will be given his second lesson when he teaches that first lesson to someone else. He, in turn, says the same thing to the one whom he teaches and so it goes with geometrical progression. They were deeply impressed as I made an English official one thirteenth literate in Hindi in twenty minutes! Since then, this movement to abolish illiteracy has gone on by leaps and bounds and promises to be an India-wide mass movement, one of the greatest movements of the age. It was characteristic that the Gaekwar was among the first to become interested, for he was progressive and enlightened.

But, on the whole, the Indian States are bulwarks of feudalism, centers of local intrigues, remnants of grinding despotism, an anomaly in the present age.

In one large State land can be had for two rupees an acre, while the same land across in British territory is worth two hundred rupees an acre. The reason is the grinding of the peasants by the officials. In that State, when a friend of mine came to divide up the produce of the land with the tenant, and the tenant saw that he was actually going to get his half share, he fell at my friend's feet and wept in gratitude. No wonder an honest official in that State said that "the attitude of the peasant is a chronic state of, No. They are beaten and have given themselves up to fatalistic despair."

In one State no one can see the ruler without offering a gold piece as Nazarana. His officials, coming to see him on tour, have to give according to their salary and position. From one such tour he came back with so much bullion that the springs of the railway carriage could not bear the weight, so an extra railway carriage had to be put on to bring it back. If that ruler sends a tray of mangoes to one of his officials, the official has to put a ten-rupee note on the tray in returning it. The mangoes would have cost, at the most, one rupee in the market! This ruler, going past a wedding celebration, told his driver to go in. When the ruler admired the wedding presents, the host's heart sank, for he knew he would have to send them to the ruler, which he did!

An official was caught in a bribery case involving forty thousand rupees. He took thirty thousand rupees of the bribe to the ruler and said, "Your Highness, of course I took this to give to you." The case was quashed and the official promoted. A compounder was dismissed by a doctor for stealing medicines. The dismissed compounder went to the ruler, gave a gift of a thousand rupees and was reinstated. The compounder's salary was twenty-five rupees per month. The ruler went to a circus and presented the circus manager with a medal. At the parting a bill was handed to the manager for the medal and the drinks, which cost him a hundred rupees.

The display of wealth amid the poverty of the masses is sickening or maddening. One ruler of a small State has three hundred dogs which cost a hundred thousand rupees a year to keep. One comparatively small State spent over two million rupees on a few days' visit of a viceroy. I went along a road where about every twenty miles was a landing field for the ruler when he went hunting in his aeroplane. A ruler has been known to go to Bombay and walk into a jeweler's shop, wave his hand, and say, "I'll take this side of the shop."

In some States the wives and daughters are not safe, especially if they be beautiful. I was told that a ruler and his retinue desired the women of a certain village. The agent of the ruler bought out the wine shop, and told the men of the village to help themselves. When the men were all dead drunk, the women were taken away. Sometimes these preliminaries are not necessary.

And now the judgment day has come. The worm, trampled on for centuries, has begun to turn. The most submissive people of the world, the Indian peasants, are now beginning to see possibilities of getting out from under their yoke of bondage. They were disarmed and so could not fight with material weapons, for the might of Great Britain guaranteed the status quo. But now Mahatma Gandhi has shown them the possibilities of passive resistance. They have the weapons within themselves! They have seen the fact demonstrated in British India of people who one day were in jail in the Non-cooperation Movement, the next day were the premiers, ministers and officials of the government. It opened their eyes. They too could do the same. They had these weapons of non-violent, non-cooperation in their hands. And a mighty weapon it is. They began to apply it through the State Congress organizations. The State Congress is a child of the National Congress but has a semiseparate existence. Every ruler today is trembling in his shoes. He has to give an account of his rule, not only to the Paramount Power but to his subjects. That moment in human history has come when men begin to reap what they have sown. A moral universe is seen in operation. Men stand before the judgment bar of God—God in the dispossessed. There is a struggle going on in every Indian State.

Rajkot, where Mahatma Gandhi fasted to make a ruler keep his pledged word, is a symptom. I was deeply interested in Rajkot, for several years ago at Rajkot, the British Resident invited in a number of the princes of Kathiawar to attend my lectures and to be his guests while doing so. A half dozen responded and went through the series of addresses on Christ and His Kingdom. The Resident wanted to invite the Europeans to the church to have me address them. The Church of England bishop refused the loan of the church—I was not in the Succession! Then the Resident invited them all to the Residency, and they came and I addressed them there, preferring this place to the stuffy atmosphere of the church.

The ruler at Rajkot, like Pharaoh under pressure of the impending revolt of his subjects, said he would grant certain reforms and then went back on his word when the pressure was relieved. Mahatma Gandhi fasted to make him keep his word—a very healthy thing. It was "the coercion of the cross" about which he spoke to me in jail. That fact set wheels of administrative machinery going, and the viceroy saved Gandhi from a fast unto death and a State from revolution.

Gandhi cannot fast to death on the doorstep of every ruler in India, but his followers will do the moral equivalent of it—they will go to jail by thousands until slumbering consciences are awakened. I have just come from one such struggle in Travancore, where the mildest people of the world are in a struggle for responsible government. I said the Travancorean is the mildest man of the world—he is. Often they will talk to you with their hand over their mouths lest they pollute your royal self with their breath, their umbrellas will often go down as you approach, and the outcaste used to step off the road at the approach of a high-caste man. I have seen a caste so low that they could not come into a town lest they pollute it, but with cloths fastened by the roadside with stones they would sit off fifty yards in the fields and beg from passers-by. All this alongside the highest percentage of literacy in India. This high percentage is largely because one fourth of the people of the State are Christians. You can stand on the hilltop of a country district and sweep your eye toward the horizon, and within that small space two hundred Christian college graduates live. That in a country district! Can that be matched anywhere in the world? And yet they had never revolted against their rulers—not until now. Joining hands with the Hindus the Christians have been going to jail, suffering for a Cause. And Christian women among the leaders! I saw the Dewan, the prime minister, and told him my views: He could put down the movement by force, but he would only drive it underground, and it would soon be back again stronger than ever. I reminded him that a wise radicalism is true conservatism, and that he who gives quickly gives ten times. I tried to mediate in the impending struggle. I felt I was the spokesman of silent millions to him. But it was of no avail. He was adamant, taking his stand on his statement in reply to Mahatma Gandhi: "Mr. Gandhi must know, of course, that it is the prince and his advisers who must determine to what extent, and when, any further steps should be taken in granting constitutional government." It is the prince and his advisers! The people who support both the prince and his advisers have nothing to say! He has given the people their text. That statement will be fought over for years to come.

For the issue is no longer a local one within the States, for with the coming of Federation, the Indian National Congress is bound to help fight out the issue of responsible government in every State. For if there is no responsible government in the States, then the representatives to the Federal Legislature would be appointed by the princes, and the National Congress would be left a minority. They, therefore, simply must fight out the issue in every State to have a majority in the supreme governing body of India. They will throw their tremendous weight into every local battle. The princes, caught between the forces of the local State Congresses and the Indian National Congress, must inevitably succumb. The future belongs to the people. The princes have had their day. They are a veriform appendix on the body of India, and the sooner they are cut out the better. For some have suppurated and are centers of poison. They can no longer talk of their rights. They have squandered their rights. They are so heavily in debt to their people that they can never pay out. The people must take over, with or without bankruptcy proceedings. The hope is that the transition will be non-violent. And if Mahatma Gandhi still morally rules India for some years to come, it will be. If not . . .?

During floods at Sitapur the water came up to the grain godown and wet the wheat. The moistened wheat

sprouted and expanded and through its silent power
pushed out the heavy brick walls from their foundations.
The floods of new thought and aspiration are rising
throughout India and moistening the dry minds and
souls of the dumb millions with new thought and aspiration. Those moistened souls are pushing against the walls
of cramping custom and autocratic rule. The wise see
the necessity of giving the masses room for expansion;
the unwise try to hold the situation by more force only
to find themselves buried amid the collapse of their rigid
and unchanging systems. It is a wise man who knows
when to yield. And many of the princes are not wise.

Down underneath the Intellectual, the Social, the Political and the Economic Revolutions is the deepest revolution of all—the Moral and Spiritual Revolution. This
Revolution is in all stages. Many lines are outwardly
holding firm buttressed by a strong communalism which
is holding beliefs long after they have inwardly lost their
grip. While many lines are being held by communalism,
nevertheless there is a real vitality in the ancient faiths.
Not far from where I am writing this, is a Hindu Center
where there are a number of British and American disciples, among them professors of universities and an outstanding surgeon. These men, weary of life, have taken
refuge in Hinduism and Buddhism. The stage of clash
between Fundamentalism and Modernism can be clearly
seen in the ancient faiths. I was talking with one of the
leaders of the Arya Samaj, Mahatma Hansraj, the founder
of the D. A. V. College of Lahore. He told me that he
had just completed the reading of the New Testament,
and the only thing he could find to object to was the story
of the killing of the fatted calf—cow-killing is a very
great sin to Hindus. (I leave out that part of the
story of the prodigal son in quoting it to the Hindus!)
But it was interesting to find that the only objection the

leader of the bitterest opponent of Christian missions, the Arya Samaj, could find was this one! Then I asked him if in Hinduism they had come to the question of whether the Vedas are vitally inspired or verbally inspired. "No," he replied, "our thought has not progressed that far." I left him and went to see Lala Lajpat Rai, a famous nationalist, and asked him if the news I had heard of his being read out of membership in the Arya Samaj was true? His reply was interesting: "Yes, I could not accept the verbal infallibility of the Vedas, so I was cut off from membership." They were trying to hold a rigid line of verbal inspiration. But listen to this professor of an Arya Samajist College speaking in one of our Round Table Conferences: "I have no respect for priests, maulvis, or missionaries. They are all a bar to progress. As there is a movement on foot to get rid of the middle man in economics so we must get rid of the middle men in religion—Krishna, Christ, Mohammed—these are the ones who divide the world into sects and clashes. The religious are not good. The only good are the purely scientific, the men who know. Religion is knowledge and knowledge is religion." There you have the situation: Men holding verbal inspiration of the Vedas, others holding a modified form of inspiration, and others belonging to the same religious organization rejecting all religion in favor of secularistic science.

All of this is taking place at the very time that there is an apparent revival of the old faiths. The old faiths have tremendous vitality and power of adaptation, but one cannot help feeling that much of the revival is whipped up by communalism as a result of national pressures. Each community is struggling for its cultural, economic, and national existence, the will to live is keeping alive the will to believe. Men who have no faith at all in their personal lives are easily whipped into a communal loyalty when any issue appears. The fact is that the roots of conviction are being cut by almost every move which the old faiths are compelled to take. All of these outer things have been sustained by philosophical roots reaching back in the Ultimate. Those roots are being cut. The idea of non-acting Brahma and the non-acting devotee are being severed from the thinking of India by the pressure of the idea of service in God and man as the highest ideal; the law of Karma operating across many births, explaining inequalities, is being replaced by the thought that we can trace within this birth the causes of inequality; the caste system is being undermined by the growing democratic thinking; the position of the Brahmin as a superior being is being knocked in the head by examination results; the idea of the world as Maya, illusion, is being replaced by the idea of the world as a very definite reality in which we must work out human destiny; the idea of the universe as a series of cycles is being replaced by the idea of progress, not *necessary* progress, but the possibility of progress if man wills it; the lower status of woman caused by Karma in a previous birth is being replaced by the thought of the worth of human personality apart from birth and sex; the practice of polygamy is being undermined by the same thought; the double standard of conduct for gods and men is being broken down by the sense of the unity and solidarity of our moral universe; the idea of religion as personal release from rebirth is being replaced by the idea of social change in this birth. And so on. All of these changes are in the direction of reform, and yet each reform is expensive in that in almost every case it cuts some philosophical root. We see, then, outer reforms taking place accompanied by steady inner decay. Said a Hindu to me: "If the rites and ceremonies that sustain Hinduism are taken away, then Hinduism will not survive a single day. We are not philosophers, so

Hinduism would have no power as a philosophy." True, but these outer ceremonies and practices have been sustained by inner ideas which have kept them alive. We are not all philosophers, but everyone holds a philosophy of life, however crude it may be. When those sustaining ideas give way, the structure falls to the ground unless held up by extraneous props. The ideas that are sustaining Hinduism and Islam are giving way, and these systems are being held by communal props. Not entirely, of course, for many ideas still hold and sustain men. But the casualties among underlying ideas are greater than the survivors.

The orthodox are trying hard to stem the tide. At Nimsar, a sacred place, pundits have pledged themselves to chant sacred verses night and day for six years, and then for six years during the day only, in order to turn back the irreligion and modernism of the present.

Most of this irreligion is among youth. They are fiercely reacting against religion which puts people to sleep regarding social injustices or arouses them to communal bitterness and strife. I went around the circle in large numbers of student groups in Lahore and had them tell where they thought the students were in regard to a religious faith. Scarcely two or three out of several hundred had any semblance whatever of a religious faith. I felt I was in the wake of a religious typhoon and that this was the wreckage. That is one picture and a very prevalent one. And yet there is this other side: I was speaking to a very skeptical university, where I knew I would have to fight for every inch I gained in the minds of the students and professors. They gave a hearing with a "pin-drop" silence. But at the close the vice-chancellor, one of the leading rationalists in India, felt he must spike what I had been saying. He had not been speaking five minutes before there was chaos. He spoke to a storm. At the close of his attempt a non-Christian student arose and said, "We would like the speaker to know that we stand with him on this matter and not with the vice-chancellor." And the students roared their applause—to my astonishment and to the vice-chancellor's! It is a very paradoxical situation, but there it is. Perhaps the students have not made up their minds which way to go. This is nowhere seen more pointedly than in the Benares Hindu University, a university founded on the attempt to combine Hinduism with modern scientific education. When I asked if this objective were being fulfilled, I was told by a high authority, "We are fulfilling the scientific side, but we haven't got around to the other as yet." The fact is, I found a very deep skepticism running through both students and faculty.

Many of the old signs are intact. But the old signs are no longer signs—they conceal rather than reveal. Said a very able judge to me: "The Brahmin is harder hit by modern life than the Moslem; the Moslem has let go his outer signs, and he seems to have succumbed to modernism, and yet he holds a core of orthodoxy in his heart— there he is still a Moslem. The Brahmin has kept all his outer signs, but on the inside he is shot to pieces—all the old inward Brahmin ideas are gone. So he is much harder hit though he seems intact." And yet the Moslem too is deeply hit.

I sat in the home of Sir Mohammed Iqbal, the great poet and philosopher, and listened with astonishment as he outlined to me his scheme of Pakistan (literally, "Holy Land"). P for Punjab, A for Afghanistan, K for Kashmir, S for Sind and Tan for Baluchistan—Pakistan, which he would carve out of North India and the Frontier for the Moslems. When I asked if they were serious about this, all the Moslem leaders, including the visiting Prince of Morocco, declared that they were. They would work the Reforms and then wait their chance to set up this Pakistan, even if it took fifty years. Politically this was interesting, but religiously one of Sir Mohammed's remarks was equally interesting: "I do not know of a single man in Islam who combines real Islam and modern education in a living blend of spirituality who could lead us at this hour." Another Moslem, a lawyer, said: "I am in a dilemma. The Persian poets have knocked the bottom out of my faith in mosques and prayers and organized religion. They tell us that only God-realization is worth while. When I turn toward this, I find that the people who say they have found God are cranks and impossible people to live with. So I am between the devil and the deep sea." "Between the devil and the deep sea" is eloquently descriptive of the condition of the modern Indian. "I am a man suspended between religions, the old is gone and nothing new has come," said a Hindu professor to me at the very seat of Hindu learning, Benares. Another Hindu, a pundit, said, "Science is making us irreligious, and it is a good thing, for it is a protest against things as they are." It is "a good thing." And this from a pundit! Many a man takes this attitude because he finds religion blocking the progress of his country. He sees what Dr. Findlay Shiras, an economist, says, "Almost all the economic evils of India come from wrong religious customs or practice." This is only partly true, for many of India's economic evils come from inside and outside exploitation, and yet many are rooted in religious customs or ideas that block reform at every point. To change India economically, a great deal of her inner thinking has to be changed, a new set of ideas that can sustain reform has to be given.

Amid these changes a great many old things are being held alongside of the new by the simple process of compartmentalization. A minister of education in a most enlightened State would not move on a journey near or far unless the kite, a kind of hawk, circled in the proper direction. He kept servants with field glasses watching for them, and when one was propitious, the servant would rush into the room where his master was immersed in educational problems and say excitedly, "Sir, now you can go." This same minister in returning from a journey would keep going round and round his house watching out of his motorcar window for the propitious kite before he would go in. A minister of education! Some highly intelligent students came to see me off at a railway station, and they wanted to put an amulet on my arm to insure me a safe journey. Students! An enlightened ruler was on his way to take over a new palace built for him, but a black cat ran across the road, and this being an unpropitious omen, he turned back and refused to enter. The palace was turned into offices instead. A ruler! When the superstitions of East and West meet in our household it is confusion worse confounded. A Hindu editor said to me, "I have the English idea that a black cat is lucky, and my wife has the Indian idea that it is unlucky, we so have many quarrels over it in our house." An editor! This is the state of tension between two outlooks—contradictory things at war. The black cats have the traditional nine lives, but eventually even cats die, and while many an ancient superstition lingers on with the tenacity of the nine-lived cat, yet they are doomed to die.

Cow dung, as a product of the sacred cow, has been used for centuries to purify floors and fireplaces by smearing it over them. The five products of the cow made into a pill purified those who had gone across the "Black Water" to a foreign land. Now in the sacred city of Benares a large industry has been built up in making cow dung into pheniel, a disinfectant. This marks the transition from superstition to science.

But there is a great deal of transition yet to be done,

for India is a land of superstitions. A very intelligent and forward-looking Indian ruler asked me to advise him on the reformation of Hinduism within his State, "For," he added, "our people have no religion, they have only superstitions." Asking a Christian missionary's advice on the reformation of Hinduism! That is not often done openly, but the inner equivalent of that is taking place all the time.

A Brahmin expatiated on the Vedanta and its universality and then went to a broken-down temple to an obscure god and offered his son's hair before the god in token of a vow. When chided with this, he replied, "We must keep up these connections with this god." Yes, connections must be kept up with dying gods and passing superstitions, but the connections are getting more and more thin. In Europe they seem to be attempting to revive dead gods. But it cannot be done—not for long, for they are dead.

Amid all the changes which are taking place in India, Christian ideas are, in large measure, ruling the development. At the very time that opposition to Christian missions—the framework in which those ideas come—is greatest, those ideas are becoming the dominant ideas in the situation. Call the roll of the reforms that are taking place in India, and if they be reforms and not reactions, you will find every reform going straight toward the Christian position—not one away from that position. That, to my mind, is most important. The ideas that rule the inner thinking of a people finally rule that people outwardly. The stage in which we are is a very mixed and confused stage and yet certain ideas clearly dominate. A Hindu said in one of my Round Tables: "I saw the difference between the three religions in a bus recently. It was crowded, and when someone tried to get into a seat where there was a Mohammedan, he objected, asserting his rights to his full space; a Hindu did not object nor would he move over—he sat unmoved; a Christian moved over and invited the man to come in. One asserts his rights; the other does nothing bad, but also nothing good; but the third actively helps. That is the distinctive difference between the three." One may or may not agree with this terse summing up by the Hindu, but one could see at a glance where the mentality was drawn and which set of ideas was dominant. Another Hindu said, "The Bhagawad Gita without the New Testament is like science without experiment." He saw that something Concrete in a world of ideas faced us in the New Testament. That Concrete Fact, Christ, is ruling the development. Even amid the most radical circles it shines out. As one of the Hindu labor leaders said: "The only ideas that can sustain our demand for social and economic justice are Christian ideas. Your faith is the only one standing up under this test." Said another Hindu, "Without Christ no religion can survive." Very often it is mixed, as in the case of a medical student: "I have three ideals—Buddha for quiet and meditation, Christ for purity and self-sacrifice, and Krishna for everyday life." He took Krishna for everyday life, for it was closest to everyday life—very like it. Another put this mixed condition in this way: "If you study the Gita, then Christ will be formed within you"—the framework was being held, but with a new content. A Hindu in Travancore will not allow his sons to hear the stories of Krishna. He insists that they get the stories of Christ in their minds in their early days. He himself allegorizes the stories of Krishna, but insists that his sons do not read them at all. Allegorization and spiritualization hold one generation, but upon the next generation they lose their hold entirely.

I know we must be on our guard against a too facile optimism. I know the deep currents of opposition to

Christianity which are running in India. I have felt the full force of them break on me. I know too the power of Hinduism to pull everything back into its bosom, after they have revolted against it. The words of Srinavasa Shastri warn us of the hobbling of Reform at every step in India: "Things begin well in India, and then they seem to be corrupted by the very air of India. Reformers come, and they end by producing only another sect. They begin by breaking down caste and end by becoming a caste." The poison in the air of India is Indifferentism, which is rooted in the idea of a non-serving, non-acting Brahma. This lays its dead hand on every reform in India, for if the heart of the universe is non-acting, then why should we be acting? "Show me your gods and I will show you your men," is profoundly true. But there is a new idea of God coming in which is supplanting Brahma. The idea of God our Father is slowly but surely becoming the idea by which India is living. It is fast becoming the working idea of God. And God, our Father, is a serving God. And Mahatma Gandhi is playing a very large part in that change. A Moslem said to me one day, "I never understood Christianity until I saw it in Mahatma Gandhi." A Moslem saw Christianity in a Hindu! Mixed? Very. But very revealing.

A Raja was arrested for his Congress activities and he said to the Christian prosecuting attorney: "We have learned from the Bible the meaning of freedom and we are arrested for teaching it. We did not learn it from our books—we learned it from your Bible." There was a great silence in the court. Men were dumbfounded. And well they might be, for it is an astonishing thing to see Christ coming into the soul of a people by a movement directed against the West.

But these days are gone, you say. The Congress movement is turning anti-Christian and pro-Hindu. Apparently, in some places. The struggle for political power may account for some of it, and the fact that the Christians were not great enough to stand entirely outside this communal struggle for power makes them get jammed between the forces in that struggle. It is a tragedy too deep for words that the Christians were divided on this matter and fell between stools. We are not good communalists and not good non-communalists. We have become like the washerman's dog—na ghar ha, na ghat ka—belonging neither to the house nor to the washing-ghat, belonging nowhere. The Christian community is caught in a political jam, but it does not belong there. It is not its natural home. It belongs to India and not to a communal scramble. Its principles make it stand for man as man and not for man as Christian. It does not have one code of morals for insiders and another for outsiders. It has one code for all men. There is nothing inherent that would keep the Christians standing in this dubious position; the real nature of its gospel will assert itself, and they should extricate themselves from this jam. If so, the present apparent hostility may subside.

The fact is that the hostility is only apparent, and largely manifest where the Christians are reactionary and antinational. Personally, I have never had greater response to my Christian message than right now. The deposit of the nationalist movement giving a Christian bias to things still remains. A friend of mine, talking to the Hindu principal of a training college, said, "The nationalist movement has brought to us two things— emancipation of women and the death of the liquor traffic." "There is a third," added the Hindu, "it has brought us Christ." Asked what he meant he said, "There has never been such a seeking for Christ as now in India." I have found this to be true. Under the surface currents this current runs deep. A Hindu judge said, "There is a common saying among us, 'We like Christ, but we don't like Christians.'" Perhaps because they can see the difference. At any rate, Christ is deeply rooted in the soul of India and will not easily be uprooted. In fact, He is becoming the force by which other things are being uprooted. "We owe much to Christianity," said the Hindu principal of a Hindu college. "Christ has become the touchstone by which we judge our institutions, our ideas, and our religions." Another Hindu put it in this way: "Hinduism is learning much from Christianity—it is learning from it to think of the untouchables and of human brotherhood. We will have to learn more from it, such as loving your enemies and of doing good to those who despitefully use you. When we assimilate more and fill in the things lacking in Hinduism, then Hinduism will be better—all right, in fact." They are trying to put the new wine of the Kingdom of Christ into the old wineskins of Hinduism. Will it burst the wineskins? It is doing it from top to bottom. For the teaching and the person of Christ are explosive and disruptive. The ferment that is going on within Hinduism now is in large measure because of the importation within that system of so many incompatible Christian ideas. They are the leaven which is sending the ferment through the whole system. Mr. Natarajan says that "the religion of the modern Hindu is an indistinguishable blend of Hinduism and Christian teaching." A Hindu nationalist spoke to us bitterly of his feelings against Western subjugation, of his deep questionings about Christian missions, and then ended up with these words: "And yet, after all I've said, I want to say that I think the Christian life is the most beautiful thing on this planet of ours. And I am in the unenviable position of a man who is trying to live the Christian life without faith in God or in Christ." Many minds and allegiances are unsettled as this from an inspector of schools indicates: "My mind has been hovering around Christ and God, but hasn't settled yet." But many have settled half way: "I was drawn toward Christianity, and my father and I used to argue in our house. He was orthodox, but was about to be converted to Christianity. But then I wondered if I couldn't find the same things in my own religion, so I turned to the national religion, where I am today." The national religion! That is the framework that holds many a doubting patriot who wants the new, but would like to have it within the national framework. Said a Hindu: "I was a skeptic, but I heard a Christian speak on 'What Christianity means to me,' and I was awakened by it and became a Brahmo Samajist." Christianity awakened him, but he too stopped in an indigenous framework. But the situation may be summed up in the words of a Hindu chairman: "When we are thinking of these things, we cannot think of a higher ideal than that of Jesus."

But there are those who feel that all this inner approach, with its half-allegiances and half-denials and its hesitations, is useless. It gets men nowhere. This, to my mind, is very superficial in its judgments. It is largely based upon the Barthian thesis that the movement up from below toward God is of the earth, earthy; only that which meets us in a crisis-demand from above is valid. This shuts off all that movement of science and of human effort of whatever kind from being of any real significance. But is God not in this upward movement as well as in the downward? I grant that in this downward movement in Christ we have God's perfect and final unfoldment and in that unfoldment our redemption. But is there no immanent Christ as well as a transcendent Christ? Is He not "the light that lighteth every man that cometh into the world"? Does He not show Himself in the upward yearnings and inner revelations as well as in the downward revelations? Must we choose between them? And if we choose only the downward, are we not compelled to discredit the movement of science and all humanitarian endeavors as being outside the movement of God's redemption? Why cannot we include them as a part of God's redemptive purpose, partial and imperfect though they may be? If not, then we doom the Christian movement to a transcendentalism which becomes in the end an obscurantism, apart from life, or only meeting it from above in a very incomplete way. I want to feel that God is in the very laws of my being, that I am inwardly fashioned for Him, and these upward yearnings are His very inspirations—yes, His very presence there. These yearnings do not supplant this perfect revelation in the historic Christ; they supplement it, and, what is more, prepare me for what I see in Him. It allows me to look on movements of science and of social betterment, not with a cold and suspicious eye, but with friendliness and eagerness and thankfulness, knowing that all this can be caught up in the purposes of the redemptive God and can be harnessed to the purposes of His kingdom. It also allows me to proclaim with more certainty and confidence the redemption in this downward movement, since I know that God is already at work in the human heart and in the movement of history. I feel that the whole of life, except the sin movement, is behind my appeal, for up and down God is moving redemptively.

I shall be grateful for any sign of His footprints in human action and in human yearnings, however imperfectly it may show Him. Give me an inch in the soul of man and I will take it and appeal for the next inch until the whole soul is laid at the feet of Christ. I am so eager for allegiance to Christ that I shall not break the bruised reed or quench the smoking flax till He hath set judgment in the earth and the isles shall wait for His law. Am I less a whole-hogger by this attitude? I am more! I would take "every project prisoner and make it obey Christ." When Professor Kilpatrick, the great educationalist, in answer to the question, What is the central discovery of modern education? replied, "He that saveth his life shall lose it, and he that loseth it for a great cause will find it," I rejoice that through the processes of education they discovered this law deeply embedded in human life, a law which is deeply embedded in the Christian gospel. True, Kilpatrick added "for a great cause," instead of "for My sake," but though that does not satisfy me, yet I shall pray and work that one day they shall see that the supreme Cause is Christ, the Cause worth surrendering to and living for and dying for. If you say He is not a Cause, but an Offer, my answer is that I take both. Because He is an Offer of God's redemption to me, He becomes through gratitude my Cause for which I shall live and die.

When Julian Huxley defines the goal of scientific humanism as the "giving of life and giving it more abundantly," I shall rejoice over the fact that through scientific Humanism men have arrived at the very statement that Jesus used as His goal: "I am come that ye might have life, and that ye might have it more abundantly." It is true that when Jesus uses "life," it must be spelled with a capital "L," and when Huxley uses it, it must be with a small one, so the difference is profound, but shall I not rejoice that men have come thus far? If in Jesus we have "a finality of direction," shall we not rejoice that men are thus turning in this direction instead of another?

Am I thereby a blind optimist and sentimentalist? Rather, I am a realist who believes in the Goal so utterly that any approach to it receives my gratitude, even though it does not get my full approval.

I therefore rejoice that Mahatma Gandhi has come so

far along the way in that he has discovered the Christian principle of overcoming evil with good and hate by love and has thereby deeply taught the Christian world. At the same time I cannot be satisfied with his stopping this side of a complete allegiance to Christ. I rejoice that Jawahar Lal has come so far along the Christian way that he is insisting on social justice to the underprivileged. But this does not make me blind to the fact that he is far short of an acceptance of Christ. But let me say this, however, that I see far more allegiance to Christ in Jawahar Lal with his demand for social justice than in those who have an allegiance to Christ but have no social passion. Heresy? So be it! To me it is appreciation of my Master who is found in reality, whether that reality be within or without the Christian Church.

I believe in mass conversions whether in mind or in outer allegiance, in spite of the fact that both of them may be only partial conversions. The fact that they are conversions toward Christ, however short of the goal they may be, is something to be accepted and rejoiced in and further converted. There are those who accept the outer mass conversions, but who look with suspicion upon the mass movement in mind toward Christ. This is inconsistent, for while both are incomplete and unsatisfactory, yet they are both toward Christ. As to which constitutes the greater step toward Him I am not prepared to say. I rejoice in both and look on both as objects of further conversion. For all allegiances to Christ, whether personal or mass, are subject to further conversions, for areas in the individual need continually to be brought under His sway.

When the head of a Hindu institution tells me that the verse that has touched India most deeply is the verse, "Father, forgive them, for they know not what they do," and asks for a picture of Christ crucified to hang in his school, I rejoice in this even while deeply conscious that it may leave the fundamental allegiances of life largely unaltered. But the Crucified is there.

When a group of Christian pastors in a certain city write to me before coming to them and suggest that I do not talk to them about such things as "forgiveness of national enemies," but instead speak to them of "spirituality," then I know that the Christ of dogma is there, but the Crucified is not there.

Both the Hindu school and the Christian pastors need conversion—which will respond to it more easily I am not sure. But the need is the same. One may define unbelief as keeping Christ out of any area of life and acting as though He were not the Son of man.

To sum up the situation: If the Christians and their teaching are only a drop in the bucket of India, nevertheless, that drop, being red with the blood of Christ, colors the whole contents of the bucket.

Under the five revolutions which are taking place in India there is need for a dynamic that will produce conversion in moral character—a character that will sustain and direct these revolutions toward constructive ends. I do not believe that dynamic can be found anywhere except in Christ. The old faiths are busy trying to save themselves, and they cannot save others. The cries that "Religion must be saved," "Religion is in danger," are symptomatic. We do not ask that Christ shall be saved. All we ask is that His saving power be loosed upon the world. That power is unspent. The difficulty is not in Him, but in the clogged channels of His coming. A Hindu at the close of a Round Table Conference said in astonishment, "If you people live what you talk about in this Round Table Conference, I don't see why you haven't evangelized the world long ago." He saw that in Christ a new hope and faith and cleansing dynamic was at work, and that if the channels were cleared out, the world would be evangelized. He was right.

Amid the Intellectual, the Social, the Economic, the Political, and the Moral and Spiritual Revolutions there is one point holding steady—Christ. He will save God to India, for our hearts can only finally worship a Christ-like God; He will save society, for the Kingdom of God is that order toward which all forward-looking social yearning consciously or unconsciously is looking; He will save life, for He puts Life into life and makes it worth while; He will save us, for He is doing it—no one else is.

It now awaits the channels to be unclogged and made adequate for His coming into the total life.

For these revolutions Christ is prepared, for He offers the ultimate Revolution—the Kingdom of God. The Christians are only partially prepared, for they have only been partially revolutionized. India is almost totally unprepared, so she stands confused. Tagore puts it this way: "In that future I saw my country a woman, like myself standing expectant. She had been drawn forth from the home corner by the sudden call of some unknown. She has had no time to pause, or ponder, or to light herself a torch as she rushes forth into the darkness ahead."

No torch—darkness ahead! That is India. No torch? Yes, there is One, and as we light the torch of India with the torch of Christ we know that our own torch shall be lighted by that very lighting.

CHAPTER V

MAKING ADJUSTMENTS
WITH NON-CHRISTIAN FAITHS

FROM the very first moment that I arrived in India I have met the attitude that all religions are the same and lead to the same goal. On that initial train journey coming from Bombay, mentioned previously, a Moslem gentleman was in my compartment. In my simplicity I knelt beside my bunk the next morning for my morning prayers. I could hear the Moslem laughing. A European (all white people are called Europeans in India) kneeling in public to pray—no wonder he laughed! It just isn't done! Only Hindus and Moslems pray in public. However, I felt that I should get to work as a missionary at once, so I read the Sermon on the Mount to my Moslem traveling companion. When I finished, I paused to see the effect of this astonishing Sermon. Surely he would bow before the shrine of such sublimity. Instead he quietly said, "We have the same teaching in our Koran." I was nonplussed. I could not debate the matter: to debate over the Sermon on the Mount is like debating over the beauty of the rose. If you see it, you see it; if you don't, you don't. But here I was face to face with the new apologetic of the non-Christian faiths. They would not try to prove your gospel is not true, but that it is not new.

This apologetic is difficult to meet, for in meeting it one seems to be narrow and dogmatic if he calls attention to fundamental differences. But surely it is just as scientific to see differences as to see identities. And if there are differences, we must honestly face them.

I have made it a policy and a principle never to attack

another man's faith in public address. I present what I have and leave him to come to his own conclusions. Again and again I am pressed by Hindus to show the differences between the faiths. I always refuse. For the moment I call attention to differences there is controversy. And Christianity cannot be seen in a controversy. But in print perhaps it can be done, for the atmosphere is calm, and men really do want to know wherein lie essential differences, for confusion is great and the need of a faith which will undergird and sustain reform and give personal resources for life was never so great. But I would not feel that I had earned the right to call attention to differences were I not at the same time calling attention to the sins and weaknesses of Western civilization and of the Christian Church.

That there are overlapping moral precepts and spiritual ideas we gladly acknowledge. But the thing we must look for is not a stray idea here and there which may be the same, but we should inquire into the sum total of outlook, tendencies, and goal.

Does Islam teach that the driving force in life is love even toward enemies, as my Moslem traveling companion suggested, or does it teach that power is the ultimate driving force? A leading Moslem once said to me: "Your hands are tied—you've got to love your enemies. We do not. We are taught to give back what is given to us. We can retaliate. You cannot." He was right in the position of the two faiths at this point. Islam is in the legal stage of development—an eye for an eye. The law of Karma is also in the legal stage—you reap what you sow, no more, no less. Now, there are three stages of development: First, the stage of unlimited revenge—you pay back as much as you can without limitation; second, the stage of limited revenge—the legal stage, an eye for an eye; third, the stage of redemption—where you overcome evil with good, hate by love, and the world by a cross of suffering for the world. The third is the most difficult, but difficult or not, it is obviously the highest. And when it is embodied in Jesus Christ, we instinctively feel that, whether we are able to attain it or not, it is the highest and the one to which we must eventually come.

A Hindu once put it to me this way: "We Hindus and you Westerners should change sacred books. We should take the New Testament, for it tells us to love our enemies; and you Westerners should take the Bhagawad Gita, for it tells us to fight—it would suit us both better." He was absolutely right about suiting us both better, and he was also absolutely right about the basic difference in the teaching of the two sacred books. "The Gita is gone," said a Hindu to me at the close of a meeting, "and you got rid of it so unobtrusively—even without mentioning it. When you showed that war is inherently wrong, then the Gita, founded on the validity of war, was undermined; it is gone." He saw clearly the difference. I once said to Mahatma Gandhi, "I can see how you could base the non-violent Non-cooperation Movement on the New Testament, but I don't see how you can base it on the Bhagawad Gita." To this he replied: "The writer or writers of the Gita wrote before mankind had sufficiently evolved to see that war is inherently wrong. But we are able to use it because we make the struggle between the Kurus and the Pandavas a moral and spiritual struggle." Mahatma Gandhi was only able to use the Gita by making its literal battlefields into moral battlefields. The difficulty with that, apart from the mental integrity involved, is the fact that between the Pandavas and the Kurus there is nothing to choose, for morally they were tweedledee and tweedledum. But the point is that between the New Testament and the Gita at this point there is a world of difference— the one is morally clear and the other is morally confused.

Even outcastes can see the difference between the gospel and other faiths at this point. Some of them, thinking of changing their faith, said, "We will become Mohammedans instead of Christians, for if we do so, then we can have revenge on the high-caste Hindus, while if we become Christians, we shall have to love them."

But the central difference is the conception of God which lies at the heart of the different systems. The most important thing to ask of one is his conception of God. For if one goes wrong at this central place of moral authority, then all life goes wrong with it. The differences at the place of the conception of God are vital differences. It is better to have no conception of God than to have a wrong conception. For life goes off at a tangent when the center goes wrong. Are all conceptions of God the same?

A Scotch pilot of a ship in Eastern waters waved all differences aside with this: "Why bother about it? The Buddhists and the Christians worship the same God. So they have the same goal." He was surprised when I told him that pure Buddhism had no teaching about God whatever—it is agnostic, if not positively atheistic. The Buddhists of Ceylon glory in the fact of their atheism and consider it better than theism.

Moreover, in Hinduism the moral law is not rooted in God. God is not the basis of morals. It is to be found in the law of Karma which operates independently of God. God is lifted above the law of Karma and has nothing to do with it. If God is lifted above morals, the devotee gets to the place where he too transcends morals. He is not affected by good or evil. Both for God and man morality has no eternal significance.

In the gospel the moral life is founded in the very nature of God. Both God and man are bound by the same moral attitudes. "Follow me as I follow God," Paul could say, and when he said this he was saying the highest thing he could say.

> "By all that God requires of me
> I know that He Himself must be."

This makes the moral universe a universe and not a multiverse. Morality has permanent meaning and does not vary from age to age and from circumstance to circumstance. What we have seen of God in Christ becomes the standard for God or man. To be Christlike is the highest attainable or even imaginable goodness. Our morality then is firm-fixed in the nature of God and in historic fact—the nature of Christ.

But this is not true of Hinduism. You are not supposed to follow the Incarnations in their moral actions. I asked a priest at a temple on which was depicted the escapades of Krishna, "Can you follow this as your own example?" "No," he said very thoughtfully; "unless you are very strong, when you come here you will go off and do the same things." The devotee's safety must lie in the fact that he is strong enough not to do what his Incarnation did.

A Gowswami (a head of a temple) once said to me regarding Krishna's doings, that while he took them literally he explained them by saying, "Ishwar [God] is not bound by the same laws as we are. Curds were His— how, then, could He steal them? Women were given by Him—how could He seduce them?" It is a great day when we see the same moral laws apply to God and man.

At question time a Hindu said this, "Is not Krishna a more complete revelation of God than Christ, for Christ only revealed the good side of God, while Krishna showed both the good and the evil? Is he not, therefore, a more complete revelation of God?" The answer was never given. I did not need to, for the crowd hissed him down.

They felt instinctively that such a thing was impossible.

Moreover, apart from the moral standards concerned, the goals are not the same. Take, for instance, the one that has the highest moral sublimity of Indian religions, Buddhism. Its goal is not at all the same as the Christian goal. The goal of Buddhism is the extinction of life; the goal of the gospel is the fullness of life. Human personality is affirmed even unto perfection. "Be ye therefore perfect, as your heavenly Father is perfect." In Buddhism human personality is denied even unto annihilation. "Is there any existence in Nirvana?" I asked of a Buddhist priest in Ceylon. "How can there be?" he replied, "For if there were existence, there would be suffering." I was talking to an Italian who had become a Buddhist monk and whose brother was a Roman Catholic priest. "My brother is praying for my soul," he said, "but the joke of it is that I have no soul!" He was correct according to strict Buddhist teaching—all one has is the result of deeds which come over from a previous birth. In attaining Nirvana one cuts the root of desire—the desire for life. Then deeds cease, and with their cessation the wheel of existence ceases to turn and one goes out into the passion-less, actionless state called Nirvana. The pulse beat of personality is extinct.

You may take your choice between the perfection of personality and the extinction of personality, but to say they are the same is to play with meanings. Mental processes cease, thought ends in mush.

And yet men say so often that all religions are the same that they have actually begun to believe it. Sometimes with hesitations. For instance, a Hindu justice of the High Court said in his remarks as my chairman, "Almost all true religions are the same." Note the hesitations—"almost," "true religions," "same." As a man who was a product of modern mushy thinking he said that they were the same, but as a jurist he had to modify his statement by "almost" and "true." It showed the confused state of his thinking. The fact is, as the Lindsay Report said, "Saying that all religions are equally true is halfway house to saying that all religions are equally false." For if you will not let me pick my values in religion, then I am through with all of them, for I find that religion *per se* has not always been a blessing to mankind—often it has been a curse. Some of the worst pages of human history have been written in the name of religion—and some of the most beautiful! I must, therefore, be allowed to pick and choose. Science does not wave its hand and say that all scientific theories are equally good. It puts the theories to the test of the facts, and the one that fits the facts best emerges as acceptable; the others are dropped aside as unfit to survive. It must be the same with religions, for they represent interpretations regarding the universe—they cannot all be true, for they cut across each other at the very fundamental conceptions of life and its meaning.

The fact is that life is rendering unfit to survive systems which do not fit into the facts. Take Theosophy, which is founded upon the idea that all religions are the same. It had its run, but now it is dying, at least in India. "Theosophy is dying," said a Hindu to me, "it has lost its drive. It has served its purpose." But why is it dying? Because the idea upon which it is founded, namely, that all faiths are the same, will not fit the facts. As soon as men began to think, the basis fell to pieces. The drive was gone. A Theosophist, a high Government official, said in one of our Round Table Conferences: "All religions are the same, but Jesus is the Son of God. However, Theosophy has taught me that some things I had given up as untrue were true." It was just at this point that Theosophy failed India; it taught India that things she was giving up as false were true. This was done by giving occult meanings to obvious wrongs. Said a Hindu to me: "Theosophy failed India. Instead of setting up a tension between its standards and our lives, making us change, it explained away obvious wrongs and let down the tension. So it morally failed us. It soothed us instead of saving us."

But note what the Government official said—"All religions are the same, but Jesus is the Son of God." But if Jesus is the Son of God, then all religions are not the same. That leads me to the very center of our problem. In an Indian State the prime minister as chairman of the meeting said, "I shall reserve my remarks for the close of the address, for no matter what the speaker says I shall find parallel things in our own sacred books." He announced beforehand that he would find them! But at the close he was nonplussed, for I did not present "things"—I presented a Person, and that Person was not found in their sacred books. Just what is the lacking thing in these and all other "books"? Just one thing—Christ! What is the unique thing in Christianity? The unique thing is not this idea, that idea, but the unique thing is Christ! When you ask me my definition of religion, I give you not a spelled-out definition, but a lived-out definition—Christ! His attitudes toward life, His spirit and life—this constitutes to me Religion. Jesus never used the word "religion," for had He done so, He would have confused the situation. He did not come to bring a religion, but to be Religion. If we are going to think in terms of God and man, we can think of nothing higher than we have seen in Jesus of Nazareth. A Man lived, and after two thousand years we can think of nothing higher when we think of God than to think of Him in terms of this Man. And this is not an imaginary Christ, but life lived out in very concrete terms. "The heavenly Krishna is pure and holy— that is the Krishna we obey," said a Hindu one day. But not so with Christ, for the earthly Christ and the heavenly Christ are one. If the Lord's Prayer says, "May Thy will be done on earth as it is in heaven," we can say with equal appropriateness, "May Thy spirit, O Christ, be shown in heaven as it was shown on earth." If it is, then we know nothing higher for heaven or earth.

"So live," said Kant, "that your actions can become a universal norm." But in saying that Kant expected of human nature more than it can bear. Who fulfills Kant's demand except Christ? The ways He took become the Way. The words He used become the Word. The life He lived becomes the Life. The truths He uttered become the Truth. Laotze said that "the Word that can be uttered is not the Eternal Word," but in Christ the word that was uttered became the Eternal Word, and became the Eternal Word just because it was "uttered." Had it not been uttered, how would we have known it was the Word? For we cannot tell whether a thing is true or not until we see whether it is operative. In Christ it was operative, verified by life. How could character be shown except in the place where character is formed—in the stream of human life? This Revelation speaks authoritatively out of life, and therefore it speaks to life.

"But," said a Hindu, "don't you shield other religions when you make Christ your definition of religion?" No, I search other religions by such a definition; for if they cannot show His spirit, it is manifest that there is no light in them. But not only do I search other religions; I search the religion built up around Christ, the religion called Christianity, which may be only more or less Christian. And not only do I search these systems, but I search our own very souls. We stand before this Judgment. The New Testament says, "We shall all stand before the judgment seat of Christ." We do now. Everything does.

Begin at this Concrete Fact and you can move out to the universal. But reverse the process and you land in skepticism. A Hindu in one of our Round Table Conferences said: "God is everywhere, in everything. We must see Him equally in all, in this carpet, in man, in the elephant. But the difficulty is that God is the Unknown and almost the Unknowable." God was everywhere—and nowhere! You cannot find God everywhere unless you find Him somewhere. I find Him supremely and perfectly in Christ. The highest thing in this universe is moral character, and the highest moral character is Christ; and if God cannot be found in the moral character of Christ, He is truly the "unknown and the unknowable." A child was drawing pictures of religious things and there was a blank space in the center. "What is that place for?" someone asked. "That is for Jesus," she replied. "Then why don't you fill it in?" "Oh, I am afraid I would spoil it," she answered. But God was not afraid to fill in the picture, and the result is,

> "A Face
>   That, far from vanish,
>   Rather grows,
>   And becomes my universe,
>   That feels and knows."

The picture of the universe was not spoiled by putting in that Face, it was saved.

But the unique thing in Christianity is not only Christ as a Person, but His message. Just what was that message? He proclaimed the Kingdom of God. Jesus went about "preaching the gospel of the Kingdom." It was the center around which everything revolved. This Kingdom seemed to be a new Order standing at the door of the lower order ready to replace it both in the individual and in the collective will with God's way of life.

This Kingdom is the most astonishing proposal ever made to the mind of man. It is universal enough to take in the sum total of human relationships, and it is intimate enough to take in my need.

Think of the Christian gospel at a time like this without this message of the Kingdom. It would stand helpless before a world need with a message not big enough to meet that need. Look at Buddhism at a time like this. Its only message is to escape from the whole order by a retreat out of life, an escape into Nirvana. Its answer is not a solution, but an abdication. No program for the reconstruction of decaying society. None whatever. Nor has ordinary Hinduism. It is quite true that with the impact of Socialism and Christianity there have come many modern movements which embody thought for the reconstruction of society. But they are not inherent in Hindu faith. Its central philosophy, the Vedanta, is that you are one with the Divine and that the world of material things is Maya—illusion. We know that the world of material things is not illusion—it is a very real world of fact pressing on us and molding us at every turn. If we do not redeem the world of material things, it will degrade us. Mahatma Gandhi has seen this necessity and has tried to fill into Hinduism some conception which will provide a program for the reconstruction of society. So he has propounded "Rama-Rajya"—the Kingdom of Rama, as the Hindu answer. But the conception cannot bear scrutiny. A Hindu writing on Rama-Rajya points out that three shady episodes in Rama-Rajya make it impossible for us to take it as our model today: The Sita episode when Rama turned out his wife Sita who had been abducted by Ravana, because Rama wanted to "satisfy the people"—to satisfy the people though his wife was innocent, and, moreover, was then about to be a mother of his child. Then again there was the incident of Rama agreeing to kill Vali when in combat with his brother Sugriva. This was done, though the combat was a challenge between brothers into which Rama stepped and treacherously ended Vali with an arrow. The third incident was of Sambuka, a Shudra. A Brahmin's son had died and Rama ordered the royal car to scour the country to find the culprit who was responsible. He found Sambuka practicing austerities in the forest and forthwith cut off his head, as no Shudra, being of low caste, had a right to practice such austerities. It was against the Shastras, the sacred books. The Brahmin boy revived when this sin against caste was thus punished. These three incidents make Rama-Rajya forever impossible as a model. And yet the world's greatest Hindu puts it forward as the basis for India's reconstruction. How does he do it? Here is a statement that lets us see the workings of his mind: "Whether Rama of my imagination ever lived or not on this earth, the ancient ideal of Rama-Rajya is undoubtedly one of true democracy in which the meanest citizen could be sure of swift justice." Justice—to Sita? to Vali? to Sambuka? But Mahatma Gandhi takes refuge in his imagination, the only place open, for the hard, bare facts preclude a literal acceptance of what happened in Rama-Rajya. The outcastes have recently staged a play depicting their position under Rama-Rajya. It showed clearly that their position was anything but desirable. No, Rama-Rajya cannot fit India's need. Said a Hindu to me: "India needs the message of the Kingdom of God, but only call it Rama-Rajya and India will take it." But the content of the Kingdom of God as taught and illustrated by Jesus is not the same of Rama-Rajya.

The Kingdom of God holds the field as the only working possibility, that is, if we are to be religious and desire at the same time to be religious with an individual and social reconstruction content. It is possible to be religious without the Kingdom of God content and framework—we can make religion communion with God, apart from any social reconstruction—but if we desire social reconstruction as well, then the Kingdom is inevitable.

A Moslem professor in the Aligarh University said this to me: "Men want a new economic order and a living God who will give moral sanctions to that order." If these are the two needs—and they obviously are—then we are shut up to the Kingdom of God. The Kingdom provides for the new economic order in that its basis is: "Distribution according to each one's necessities" (Acts 2. 45). A better basis you cannot find. To the end of time "to each according to his need" will be the basis and the only basis. In the present order the basis is: To each according to his greed. This is an impossible basis resulting in a jungle civilization. The new economic order is provided for in the Kingdom of God. Moreover, there is the living God in this conception giving moral sanctions to that Order. The kind of God Jesus shows in the Kingdom of God is a God who not only gives moral sanctions to the new Order by adequate commands and regulations, but is, by His very nature, the basis of that new Order. The new Order is based on His nature and not merely on His commands. His nature is that of a Father—hence the cooperative order inheres in Him. The organization of the world as a family is inherent in the nature of God as a Father. The Christian solution of the world's problems is simple. It proposes that the family spirit, which is the cooperative spirit, be projected beyond blood relationships to human relationships—straight out into the economic, social, and political relationships. It won't work, you say? Won't work? It is the *only* plan at work today on a wide scale. The family is the most widespread human unit, and there the love motive is the organizing principle, resulting in a cooperative order. It *is* working, the one unit that is keeping alive the soul of the race. Take out that cooperative unit and the human race will sink back into barbarity overnight. The Kingdom of God principle, then, is working, working on the widest scale of any principle and is the very soul of the race. What is needed is to break the bonds, enlarge the family, and make the family principle operative in the sum total of human relationships. We are not asking for the introduction of a new principle, but only for the deepening and enlarging of a principle already at work on the widest scale of any principle now operative. "I beseech you by God, the Father, after whom every family in heaven and earth is named." God sets the basis and standard in His own character for the Family, and that same principle is now operative within good human families. We are building on foundations deeply laid in the nature of God and in the very structure of human society where that society is a society and not a jungle relationship. This, then, is the taking of the truly natural and making it part and parcel of the supernatural. The supernatural Father has laid the foundations of His Kingdom in the very structure of natural human living, the human family, and His Kingdom is the extension of that family spirit, which is the spirit of love, into the whole of human living. You may take it or leave it, but this is the Rock upon which we must build in the future or upon which we must go to pieces. It is the profoundest foundational idea ever presented to the human race and ever embodied in that race as a working principle.

Moreover, that principal of love is not merely in the nature of God and not merely embedded in the human family. We see it at its perfection in the character of Jesus Christ. His character is the Key to the meaning of the Kingdom of God. The Kingdom of God is Christlikeness universalized. It is the spirit of Christ operative in human affairs.

When Peter confessed, in behalf of the disciples, that Jesus was the Christ, the Son of the living God, Jesus replied that Peter thereby had the keys to the Kingdom of God. How? In the crude fashion that he stands at the heavenly gate to let people in? Hardly. In recognizing Jesus as the Christ, the Son of the living God, he had within his hands the key to the Kingdom—Christ Himself was the key. If you want to understand what the Kingdom is like, look at Him; He is the embodiment of that Kingdom, the key to its nature and the illustration of it in action. He used the phrase "for the Kingdom's sake" and "for my sake" as synonymous. They are synonymous, for He is the Kingdom personalized.

When He went on and said that whatever Peter loosed on earth, should be loosed in heaven, and whatever he bound on earth, should be bound in heaven, He meant that this Kingdom, of whom Christ was the Key, is so basic that heaven and earth are ruled by the same laws—these laws are of a piece—the judgments of earth are the judgments of heaven, the bound on earth are bound in heaven, the Kingdom and its laws are one, both for heaven and earth.

When we see the Kingdom of God looking at us through the eyes of Jesus, then we know that we are face to face with ultimate Fact—something that is valid in heaven and on earth, and for time and eternity. If Jesus Christ is not the Key to God and man and to the organization of human relationships, then there is no key. A pupil said of a beloved teacher, "He always threw down in front of us a bunch of keys." Christ did just that. He threw down Himself as the Key to human and divine living. If He isn't the Key, then God has thrown down

before us a Chinese puzzle to which there is no answer—
the symbol of life is a Sphinx.

Said a young professor in one of our Round Tables:
"Everything is gone except the character of Jesus Christ.
I hold to that. But that is all I have." But with that he
had the Key to everything in heaven and earth. Turn
that Key, act on Him, and see if everything in heaven
and earth does not come out right.

But without this Key we are like the modern economists
of whom it is said that "they are like Columbus, who set
out not knowing where he was going, not knowing what
country he had discovered, and when he came back, he
did not know where he had been." Men are confused
when they begin with any key other than Christ. An
army officer looking over a shelf of books at the Ashram
saw one entitled, *The Problem of God,* and he quietly
and naïvely remarked, "Is there a problem?" There
wasn't to him. He had found Christ. The problem of
God was no longer a problem but a possession. "How
goes the battle?" I asked of a queenly lady who had just
entered into a victorious experience of God. "There is
no battle," she replied with quiet assurance. There
wasn't, there was only victory—all down the line.

When I arose from my knees at the time of my conversion, I grabbed someone near me and said, "I've got it."
Why "it"? What did I mean by "it"? Well, as I look
back I see it was the only word to use. By "it" I meant
that intangible something after which the human race is
reaching—completion, integration, wholeness, fellowship
with God, peace with oneself, power to face the future,
release from what one has been and done, the new Order
—in other words, *It.* That "It" comprehended everything
one wanted in heaven and on earth.

A Hindu chairman said at the close of one of my addresses, "When we hear him, we hear the notes of Buddha,

of the ancient sages, of Positivism, of Humanism—all these seem to be blended in his message." And yet I had mentioned none of them. I had presented Christ and Christ alone. Why had he heard all these? Because in Christ there is "It"—that something for which men have been seeking through many systems, many roads, and many persons; and when they find It, they know the search is at an end—this is *It*.

Another Hindu chairman expatiated on the stability of India's religions and how they had a living core within them, and then ended by saying, "But, of course, there is nothing more beautiful and higher than the Spirit of Jesus." Men may expatiate all they will on all the subjects they please, but in the end they come out at the place of Christ—for He is *It!* You are bound to end up there if you go far enough with life.

A friend of mine was explaining the cross to a Hindu who was an atheist. A Moslem listening said: "You don't know what you are doing. You are degrading God and blaspheming Him when you say He suffers." "No," replied the atheistic Hindu. "If we are to believe in any God at all, we must believe in the kind of God Jesus shows." The atheistic Hindu knew instinctively that this was *It*. There was no arguing. Can you argue with the eye that sees the light?

Said a very able Hindu to an audience at the close of one of my addresses: "I firmly believe that the ideal and example set forth by Jesus Christ in His life is the ideal toward which the world is slowly but surely progressing. History points to it. And I am sure a time will come when the world will be a Christian world, not in the external and dogmatic sense; that is, of going to Church and taking baptism, but in the real sense, namely, by following and living up to the ideals which the Lord Jesus Christ exemplified to perfection in His life." That was said before the present wholesale slipping away on the part of the world from the principles of Jesus Christ and a mad rush toward jungle ethics and attitudes. But this cannot last. The words of Francis Thompson are literally true: "All things betray thee, who betrayeth Me."

The world situation is deteriorating to the degree that we slip away from Christ—all things are betraying us, for we are betraying Christ. It may be that sorrow and self-inflicted pain shall yet "toss us to His breast."

The words of the Hindu will yet come true, for we live only as we live according to His way. A Bahaist lady from the West came to India and said to an audience: "When the sun rises it rises in the East—Lux ex Oriente —and comes through window after window of the house. Each window represents a religion and each religion thinks it has the light. Jesus was a window and Buddha was a window, but there is one Sun shining through them all." Her Parsee interpreter took issue with her in these words: "I beg to differ from the lady. Christ is not just a window—He is the light shining into these windows. He is the Sun itself!" The Parsee was right. There is no category in which we can bracket Him with others. He rises above saint and sinner in sinless grandeur. If He represents man, then I am not yet a man; I am subhuman.

The one perfect possession of the Christian Church is Jesus Christ. He is unique not only in the absence of sin, but in the perfection of moral virtues which meet in Him —every virtue balanced by its opposite virtue; His passivity balanced by His militancy; His world-renouncing with His world-participating; His self-denial with His self-assertion; His love of God with His love of man; His moral grandeur with His humility; His mastery with His servant-of-all attitude; His purity with His approachableness; His mysticism with His practical service; His terribleness with His tenderness; His law with His grace.

He is the Unique Christ. And, as we have seen, His message of the Kingdom of God is unique. There is simply nothing else like it on the horizon. We can still be missionaries of such a Christ and of such a Kingdom.

So amid the changes of the years I have remained unchanged at this point. I am still a missionary with all the consent of my being, more certain now than I was when I started, thirty-two years ago. The clashes of the years have but driven the conviction deeper, till now I no longer hold it—it holds me.

To hold that all religions are the same is to practice mental abdication. This is not mental liberality; it is nonsense—and unscientific. Science does not wave its hand over all theories and say they are equally good and equally valid. That attitude would paralyze science and stop its progress—its wheels clogged in a mass of contradictions. Science puts its theories under life to see whether they will fit the facts. It does not say the Copernican and the Ptolemaic theories are equally good. It chooses. And in that choice there is progress. We too must choose in the deepest things that concern life. I do choose. I choose Christ and His Kingdom. It is not faith that makes men believe in everything. It is a false tolerance which is really Indifferentism—my old haunting word come back again.

An astronomer working in a Government observatory was seen by his superior officer worshiping the dragon that had swallowed the sun at the time of eclipse. When asked how he, an astronomer, a believer in science, could believe in this story of the dragon he replied, "I believe in both." Really he believed in neither. Mental Indifferentism was his creed. This reminds me of a description of Theosophy which a Hindu gave: "It is a creed which gives you the privilege of praising all religions without the obligation of obeying any one of them." When you make your choice, you have to obey the one you choose, but this Indifferentism leaves you free to do nothing and at the same time feel the sense of satisfaction at being broad and liberal.

This Indifferentism is often found among Christians and even among missionaries. I was told by a missionary lady that we had no right to try to convert people—but she forthwith began to convert me to chrysanthemums! She was enthusiastic and would have me believe hers were the most beautiful in the station. They were. And she was their glowing evangelist preaching the gospel of chrysanthemums! Men who try to convert the East to a brand of tobacco—"A cigarette in every Chinese mouth" is the slogan—often object to our converting people to Christ and His Kingdom. Well, I take my choice and pick my values. And I have no apology in trying to convert people to them.

"What is the object of these lectures? What are you trying to do? Convert us?" asked a Hindu at question time. "Of course I am," I replied, "what do you think I am here for if not to convert you? But I am convertible, and if you have something better than I have, I am a candidate for conversion." They laughed and we were friends. They expected me to apologize, but respected me when I did not. "Thank God for somebody who believes something," said a Columbia University student as he came away from a meeting. He was tired of sitting on the horns of a dilemma and was grateful for someone who dared choose. When I said to a Hindu audience that I was convertible, one Hindu arose and said, "Yes, but you would be a very hard nut to crack." I replied: "Well, I suppose I would be, but not for the reason you think. It is not superior intelligence, I know that. The reason probably is that I no longer hold my faith—it holds me."

And I propose to share that faith while there is breath within me.

But just what is the goal of the evangelism we are aiming at? I would define it as follows: The task of evangelism is the realization of the eternal Kingdom of God in time and on earth both in the individual and in the collective will; this Kingdom embodied in and become personalized in Christ who in His life, teaching, death and resurrection becomes the key to the meaning of that Kingdom and the way into it through the new birth—this new birth bringing one into the Church, which is the fellowship of those devoted to the purposes of the Kingdom.

CHAPTER VI

ADJUSTING ONESELF TO MAHATMA GANDHI

As one walks along the Indian Road he soon senses the fact of a very dominant figure on that road whether he be present or whether he be absent—the figure of Mahatma Gandhi. Mahatma Gandhi sums up the paradoxes of India. He is the retiring saint who directs public affairs; he is one of the world's meekest men who is dictatorial to an astonishing degree. He is not a member of the Indian National Congress, but nothing important is done there without his consent. He is the world's greatest pacifist who bases his pacifism on the Bhagawad Gita, which teaches that war is right. He would go back to cottage industries, and yet has followers who are Socialists and would capture and develop this power age and use it for human justice and advance. He is one of the most universalized of men, and yet counts himself a Sanatanist Hindu, the ancient orthodox. He is a Hindu, a real one, and yet many people call him a Christian, a real one. He cleans latrines, and yet Brahmins vie with the multitudes to get sight of his sacred person. He is gentle and yet a man of iron. He has the method which the world desperately needs, and yet the world can't get at it, for it is wrapped in strange wrappings. He seems to gather in his own person the meaning of the Indian Road, for he is the meeting place of the old and the new. He is the ancient ascetic come to life again—the man who can renounce. India has always loved the man who could give up things. But India does not now love the renounced person in an unqualified way. The ascetics are slipping in their hold on India. Jawahar Lal Nehru says they are one of the incubuses on the soul of India which must be

119

eliminated. But India still has a love for those who can sit lightly to this world. Maharajas in their glittering splendor do homage to them. But there is now this qualification: the ascetic must renounce for a purpose. He must give up in order to serve. For the new ideal of service linked to religion has come in largely with Christianity. A Hindu landowner tried to get a Maharaja to do a certain thing for the low castes. Finally he succeeded. His comment was, "Well, it was the Christian thing to do." A Hindu feels that this service to the outcastes was the Christian thing! This spirit of lowly service to the underprivileged is undoubtedly identified with Christianity, and yet its most gripping and dramatic illustration has come through a Hindu. It has gripped the mind of India. The old ascetics do not serve. Why should they? They must become like the non-serving Brahma. To serve would take them away from *It*. But that ideal is fast losing ground in the soul of India. The most modern Vedantists, the Rama Krishna Mission, are dedicated to service. India wants in religion something linked with the reconstruction of their country. Mahatma Gandhi is the meeting place of these two ideals—the ideals of renunciation and service. India sees in him its ancient ideal and this new ideal in a living blend. Hence his hold upon the affections of those of the old and of the new mentality. He is India, old and new, incarnate in one person. He is the meeting place of movements, and hence his significance beyond his own person.

When I told a Hindu that one of my books was entitled, *The Christ of the Indian Road,* he inquired, "Is it on Mahatma Gandhi?" He thought Mahatma Gandhi to be the Christ of the Indian Road—Christ in an Indian setting. There are many things in Mahatma Gandhi that do remind one of Christ. I have the feeling that the greatest things in Mahatma Gandhi are Christian things.

The fundamental note in his life—the overcoming of evil with good, of hate by love, of wrong by taking on oneself suffering, of conquering by a cross—is essentially a Christian note. There is no clear authentic note of this kind in the ancient faiths. But after that is said, one must add that, although Mahatma Gandhi is deeply Christianized, far more so than most Christians, yet he is essentially a Hindu. The center of his allegiance is not in Christ, but in the Gita. He has made his choice, and his choice did not fall on Christ, but on the Krishna of the Gita. I say Krishna of the Gita and yet I am not so sure that this is entirely correct, for Rama is often on his lips and apparently the center of his affections. Perhaps there is a bi-polarity in his thinking—the Gita for its teaching and Rama for his person.

I am not sure he loves Krishna, but he loves the Gita and makes it his refuge. "I do not turn to the Sermon on the Mount but to the Bhagawad Gita for consolation," he told a missionary audience in Calcutta. Mahatma Gandhi is a Hindu for the center of his allegiance is Hindu.

And yet he has difficulties about a full allegiance to the Gita. He finds his own moral and spiritual life greater than the basis of his faith. Not that he would say so, but the outside observer can see that this is so. Witness his statement to me on the Gita and war.

Mahatma Gandhi is a Hindu like many another Hindu —a Hindu with reservations and explanations. One Hindu said regarding the Gita, "We can best follow Sri Krishna, not by getting his verses by rote and repeating them to others, but by interpreting them in the light of our own experience and when necessary improving on them, and even putting them aside in a spirit of reverence even as Krishna did the Vedic religion" (I. S. R. January 7, 1933). "Improving on them and even putting them aside"—this is what Mahatma Gandhi has been compelled to do, for his spiritual life is greater than its basis, the Gita. He got the foundations of his spiritual life in the gospel and in Tolstoy, and when he superimposes this on the Gita basis, it does not fit. He is driven then into contradictions and explanations that do not explain. A Hindu says of Sri Krishna: "He did many tricky and underhanded things to get the Pandavas the Kingdom, but then the end justifies the means." This Mahatma Gandhi cannot accept, for he does not believe that the end justifies the means. He is too inherently honest for that. Said a Hindu Chairman at Guntur: "Buddhism did not believe in God, so was unsuited to India. Krishna was not a reformer. He left things as they were. He gave the people what they wanted. But Christ was a reformer and a revolutionary." "He left things as they were"—and, worse, he left things as they ought not to have been! A Hindu professor in Bombay testifying before a court was making a case for extramarital relationships with women and trying to prove that virginity was not necessarily a good thing, cited Sri Krishna as an example of adultery being right. The judge was horrified. This brings on a moral embarrassment, and great and pure souls like Mahatma Gandhi have to turn a blind eye to this side of things in order to accept the other part of the teaching of the Gita which really appeals to them. But there is an inner embarrassment accompanied by many explanations.

The only explanation that one can give of this fact that Mahatma Gandhi can be so straight on great moral issues and be so different when it comes to the religious side of things is probably in the fact of his doctrine of Swadeshi. It was first applied to the use of one's own native goods, but is now applied to one's religion—one is to take the dharma, or religion, of his native soil and not that of another. "Better is one's own dharma badly done, than that of another well done," says a verse in the

Gita. This has been broadened from a reference to caste duty, or dharma, to one's religion in general. One should not exchange his own native faith for any other. "The confusion of dharma is the cause of all confusions," says another passage in the Gita. Mahatma Gandhi links this thought with his strong nationalistic feeling and identifies national feeling with Hindu dharma. It is quite true that he says that he has great reverence, even an equal reverence, for both Islam and Christianity, but one can see that his working principle of life is a Hindu nationalism.

One can sympathize with this, for it is a natural attitude for a subject race to take. In the field of politics and economics a subject race is subject to the interests of the dominant power. How deeply that iron of domination has gone into the soul of India only an Indian really knows. Mahatma Gandhi once wrote to me in answer to my urge that he should not launch his civil disobedience movement: "You have no notion of the wrong that this government has done and is still doing to the vital part of our being." But in the field of religion their souls are their own. "We must hold to our religion, for it is the only thing we have left," said a Hindu to me one day. So religion is identified with nationalism. India is making a case for Swaraj, and she must assert herself against the world, but in the field of religion she feels she has her past to turn back to.

Of course there is an ever-increasing Socialist group which deplores this turning to the religious past. One Hindu youth said, in disgust, "After we gave the reins of power into Mahatma Gandhi's hands at the last session of the National Congress, the first thing he did was to dedicate an idol temple in Delhi." But when Mahatma Gandhi insists on Swaraj in religion, he is a child of his circumstances. Placed as he is, it is difficult for him to take any other position. But it has been a very great loss to the world that he has had to take it. I am persuaded that Mahatma Gandhi could have led us in East and West on the question of war had he not been bound up with Swadeshi Hindu mentality. When the world needed him and was prepared to follow him, he became more and more a Sanatanist Hindu, and there the world could not follow him. Along in 1923 Mahatma Gandhi came out of jail after his first imprisonment. He made an appointment for me to see him at 6 A. M. in the Poona hospital, where he had been operated on by a British surgeon and lovingly attended by British nurses. As I paced the station platform asking God for a message to Mahatma Gandhi I threw open my Bible for a message. I know how precarious this method of getting guidance is, and it is not my accustomed way of getting it, but I was in a tight corner and needed help. And God does help the simple-minded. I am sure He helped me. The passage which my eyes fell on in opening my Bible was the account of the disciples asking Jesus if He would at that time restore the Kingdom to Israel. They, as nationalists, asked for the restoration of their national sovereignty and He promised them a greater Kingdom extending from Jerusalem to the ends of the earth if they would be witnesses unto Him. They asked for the small and He offered them the world-wide. I saw the parallel between the disciples' and Mahatma Gandhi's positions. When I went in, I asked him to give me a message to the West, a message on how we, as Christians, should live this Christian life. He thought a moment and then said: "A message like that cannot be given by word of mouth, it has to be lived. The only thing I can do is to live it." I replied that I thought he was right, but if he had no message for me, I felt I had one for him and quoted my passage and drew the parallels. I pointed out that the disciples of Jesus and he were both wanting Swaraj, and I deeply sympathized with him in it and hoped he would get it, and believed that it would come sooner or later; it was a question of time. But here was a greater Kingdom, a world-spiritual Kingdom, awaiting him if he would take it. We of the West were sick of the methods of militarism, but were in a vicious circle and did not know how to get out. He, as the apostle of the non-violent, could get us out if he would. If he would step out, he could lead us in both East and West. We were ready for that leadership. But there will have to be a basis for this world revolt against militarism, and the New Testament provides it. If he would, therefore, come out and give his clear witness to Christ, he could lead us in East and West. I added that I did not talk about his being a technical Christian in the sense of baptism and the Christian Church, I would leave that with him, but I did plead that he give his clear witness to Christ, as the center of his allegiance and of the movement. Thus he could lead us. He did not answer me then. But the world since then has had his answer. He would be a Sanatanist Hindu and would found his witness on the Gita. He renounced his world-spiritual Kingdom for a local one. He would be Swadeshi. He has, therefore, failed to lead the world in the present crisis. He is an interesting figure, the world's most interesting figure in many ways, but it is difficult for him to rise above the local Hindu situation. In becoming more and more a Hindu, he has lost grip upon the Moslems except upon a comparatively few Congress Moslems. The singing of "Bande Mataram," the national song, one verse of which is to Kali, a Hindu goddess, is a symptom of the Hindu tinge to the Swaraj movement. Because of an outcry on the part of Moslems and Christians, this Kali verse is now being suppressed, but the fact that it was naturally taken as a part of Swaraj is symptomatic.

Mahatma Gandhi has been caught in this movement—

in fact, is the soul of it, and therefore is unable to lead us as a world figure. After a lapse of fifteen years I appealed to him again on this point, urging him to go to Europe and make an appeal for peace as we drifted toward a world war. I reminded him of what I had said before and said that I was still convinced that he could lead us out of war. His reply was illuminating:

"As to your second suggestion, I have no inward call. I feel that even in India itself my mission is far from being fulfilled. Though non-violence has made some headway, it has not proved enough to make India a pattern of peace as I have pictured it to myself. There is much violence in the air, as witness the riots that take place here and there. We have frequently to depend upon the police and sometimes even the military. It gives me no satisfaction to know that such things must happen in a big country like India, which is almost a continent where the biggest national organization claims non-violence as its settled policy. It must acquire control over forces of violence before it can appear before the nations of the world as a messenger of peace. I am quite clear in my mind that my work lies in India. Perhaps if I succeed here, I won't need to go out of India to preach peace; and I know if I went out today, my word would lack power."

It is a beautiful letter, but it plainly shows that he is caught in the web of the Hindu situation and cannot get out. Not even in India. He complains that the Hindu-Moslem clash in India precludes him from speaking with authority in the world situation. But his becoming more and more a Hindu also precludes his becoming a mediating force in India between Moslems and Hindus, for the Moslems on the whole do not trust him. They feel that he is standing for a Swaraj that is essentially Rama-Rajya, a Hindu Swaraj. He is not, I know. But he is caught in a vicious circle—he cannot lead the world because he is becoming more and more a Hindu. He cannot lead in the healing of the Hindu-Moslem breach in India for the same reason. He cannot lead the world because he has not succeeded in India—the vicious circle is complete; he is caught—a supreme tragedy. For I am absolutely convinced that he has the method which the world is in need of—the method of non-violent, non-cooperation. It is the moral equivalent of war, and if applied on a large scale, it could lead us out of war. The country that adopts it will assume the moral leadership of the world. India came near doing it. Had she been great enough to have kept to it, she would today be leading us.

George Landsbury, one of the world's great Christians, replied to me when I asked him about the question of applying the Gandhi method to Japan, the method of non-violent non-cooperation, the moral equivalent of war, "How can you have a moral equivalent of an evil?" My reply is that while war is centrally evil it has enough good around it to float it in the minds of many people. Patriotism, cooperative effort, comradeship, willingness to sacrifice for a cause, the desire to protect the weak—these are the good things clustering around a central evil. Gandhi's method is the moral equivalent of these good things, minus the central evil of hate and killing.

Rajendra Prashad, one of the men who has caught Mahatma Gandhi's spirit most deeply, said at a flag-raising, "This Swarajist flag is the only flag that stands for the acceptance of suffering instead of the giving of suffering." And I agree. It is magnificent. And the world needed it. But Mahatma Gandhi could not give it to us. He had chosen a framework which narrowed it and made it difficult of world-acceptance.

Not that Mahatma Gandhi has not a right to choose to be a Hindu. He has the same right that I have to be a Christian. But the Hindu basis is bound up with so much that we cannot take, that Mahatma Gandhi, holding the precious jewel of non-violent non-cooperation in that setting, fatally prejudiced it before the world. He might have been the outstanding prophet of this age—he has chosen to be a Sanatanist Hindu, still great and still noble, but limited by that choice.

Not that I should want to narrow him into a denominational acceptance of Christianity. Not that. Someone quoting me said that "Stanley Jones does not want Mahatma Gandhi to be a Christian." What I did say was that I did not want him to be a Methodist. Unfortunately, those two terms are not always synonymous! I'm not sure what we would do with him as a Methodist! He would break all our molds. He is really too great for them. But what I really do want him to be is a Christian, a man who makes Christ the center of his trust, his loyalty and his affections. I say this, for I feel that he belongs there. When he is himself, the real Gandhi, he is a Christian in his whole outlook and spirit. It is only when he is India-conscious and politically-conscious that he seems to be a Hindu. My prejudices? Perhaps. But my conviction is that Mahatma Gandhi is naturally a Christian, he is unnaturally a Hindu. When he gives vent to his real nature, he speaks in Christian terms and acts in a Christian way. The Hindus themselves have felt this, as one expressed it, "There has been one Christian in the world—Christ; and India is about to produce another—Gandhi." Only the Mahatma's assurances that he was a Hindu have convinced them that he is a Hindu. Everything else said he was a follower of Christ.

But the crucial question arises: Would it make any difference if Mahatma Gandhi were a follower of Christ? That very question was raised in the Jerusalem Conference by an Indian who said, "Before this Conference can go on with any degree of reality it must answer the question, Would it make any difference to Mahatma Gandhi if he were a Christian?" He raised a most crucial question. If it would not, then Christ is not necessary to all men. Some men, as Mahatma Gandhi, have outgrown the necessity for Christ. And if he is not necessary for all men, then he is not necessary for any man. A thing which is not universal is not true, for truth by its very nature is universal.

My answer to this question is a straight categorical Yes, it would make a difference, a very great and fundamental difference. He would find God in immediate experience. Now he is convinced of God, believes in God, and acts upon that belief, but a vivid personal experience of God he lacks. "I have not seen Him, neither have I known Him, but I have made the world's faith in God my own." I wonder if the simplest Christian coming through Christ to God does not go further than that. He finds an experience of God which is immediate and experimental. "After a search for over forty years I have no such assurance as you say you have," wrote Mahatma Gandhi to Mrs. J. R. Chitambar. Are the Christians, then, better than Mahatma Gandhi? We do not claim that; we only claim that they have a better Way, a Way which works. We find God in Christ, or, rather, God finds us in Him.

I once poured out my heart to Mahatma Gandhi in this letter: "You know my love for you. I have tried to interpret you and your movement to the West. I had thought that you had grasped the center of Christianity. But I am afraid I must change my mind. You have grasped certain principles which have molded you and have made you great, but I do not feel that you have grasped the person of Christ. Here you are weak. You said in Calcutta that you do not turn to the Sermon on the Mount for consolation, but to the Bhagawad Gita. Neither do I turn to the Sermon on the Mount for consolation. I turn to this

Person who embodies the Sermon on the Mount; but He is much more. In Him principles look out at me with tender eyes. Here I think you are weakest in your grasp. You have grasped the principles but have missed the Person. I beg of you to penetrate through the principles to the Person and come back and tell us what you have found. I do not say this as a mere Christian propagandist, I say it because we need you and need the interpretation which you could give if you really grasped the center of the Christian faith, the Person of Christ."

His reply was immediate and illuminating: "I appreciate the love underlying your letter and kind thought for my welfare, but my difficulty is of long standing. Other friends have pointed it out to me before now. I cannot grasp the position by the intellect; the heart must be touched. Saul became Paul not by an intellectual effort, but by something touching his heart. I can only say my heart is absolutely open, I have no axes to grind. I want to find truth, to see God face to face. But there I stop. Do please come to the Ashram when you have the time."

This is a characteristic letter, straightforward and clear and frank. What a master of straightforward English he is! There are two illuminating facts in that letter. First, he recognizes that he has not found something, that there is something he is missing. Second, that something is to be found not by an intellectual effort, but by a heart-experience. That something the simple, sincere Christian finds through Christ. He finds God. It works.

Therefore, I want Mahatma Gandhi to be a follower of Christ both for his sake and the sake of the world. I repeat that I am not interested in his joining one of our denominations, or even of accepting Christian baptism, though I believe in both, and I baptize people when they want it and am assured they are Christ's, but I am deeply interested in his centering his allegiance in Christ and giving that witness to the world.

A great many people come to India and ask Mahatma Gandhi some very foolish questions. Among the most foolish questions ever asked of him was this one: "What do you think of Stanley Jones?" To which the Mahatma replied: "He is a very sincere man, and a very earnest man, but he is too certain about religion. He, therefore, lacks humility." From Mahatma Gandhi's standpoint he was right. He believes that salvation is an attainment through one's own disciplined efforts. If so, then, of course, one may not speak of it; it is one's own, and to speak of it would be indelicate, would lack humility. But I looked on salvation, not as an attainment, but an obtainment, the gift of grace. I had nothing to offer save my bankruptcy and, to my astonishment, Christ took me, forgave me, and sent my happy soul singing its way down the years. I could speak of this, for it wasn't mine—it was the gift of Another. In speaking of it I was simply laying the tribute of my gratitude at the feet of Christ, my Saviour. Not to speak of this would be indelicate, for it would be acting as though what I had found was my own.

From Mahatma Gandhi's standpoint he was right, from my standpoint I was right, and I think I was a little righter than he was! For he was taking the way of works and I was taking the way of grace. The way of grace brings certainty, realization; the way of works brings unsatisfied striving, uncertainty. This is true both in East and West. It is the difference between the evangelical and the legalistic attitudes.

I first met Doctor Ambedkar, the leader of the outcastes, in jail about five years ago. Neither he nor I were permanently there! We had both gone to see Mahatma Gandhi. When Mahatma Gandhi introduced me to

Doctor Ambedkar, I remonstrated against taking his time from Doctor Ambedkar. "His is a life-and-death struggle and my questions are comparatively academic," I said. "No," replied the Mahatma in his gracious way—and how gracious a man he is! He disarms you. People come to him with blood on their horns and go away tamed and charmed at his gracious smile and open frankness. "No," he said, "Doctor Ambedkar and I agreed that we would talk till you came and then we would suspend our conversation and he would listen in as you and I talked." I reminded him of the things on which he and I agreed regarding the outcaste movement and then came to the points on which I was puzzled. "First, how is it that you are trying to do away with untouchability, but are leaving caste intact? There are the four castes, the Brahmin, the Kshatriya, the Vaisaya, and the Shudra, while under these are the outcastes with no standing within caste. You undertake to wipe out the outcastes and put them up one rung higher within the caste system. It is a matter of degree, not of kind. You raise them one rung, but you leave the caste system intact with these outcastes embodied in it. You still visualize society this way (holding my four fingers vertically), while I visualize society this way (holding my four fingers horizontally), all men equal." "So do I," said the Mahatma. "Then caste is gone," I replied. To which he answered, "Yes, but there are differences which come over from a previous birth which make for differences in human qualities." So he did justify a modified form of caste based on inherent qualities. He defended it though he himself does not keep it.

"Second, I don't see why you get the outcastes to go into the temples of which the Brahmin is the head. Are you not fastening the yoke of Brahminism on the untouchables by throwing the weight of the untouchables behind the Brahmins, their traditional oppressors?" At this

Doctor Ambedkar and his outcaste retinue seated with him laughed. The Mahatma replied, "After all, the Brahmin is not as bad as he has been made out to be. He has been the protector of Hinduism through the centuries." Here he did not face fairly the issue I raised, and instead fastened on his evident point of interest, the protection of Hinduism. I asked about the protection of the outcastes and he replied in terms of the protection of a system.

"Third, haven't you better phases of Hinduism to which you can introduce the outcastes, better than temple Hinduism? After all, the temples are the centers of idolatry, and idolatry has been the mother of superstition in all ages." His reply: "What the mosque is to the Moslem and the church is to the Christian, so the temple is to the Hindu. Besides, there is idolatry in all religions, Islam and Christianity as well." To which I replied, "Well, if idolatry is inherent in all religions, then I am through with them all, for I am against idolatry as such." "But," said the Mahatma, "don't you have an image in your mind when you go to God?" "Yes," I replied, "I do, but it is a moral and spiritual image, an image of God which I get from Christ, an image, therefore, which I believe represents God and does not misrepresent Him as idolatry does, for I believe that God is a Christlike God." To this there was no reply.

"Fourth, when you fast to get your view across on people, is it not a form of coercion?" "Yes," he replied, "the kind of coercion that Jesus exercises upon you from the cross." To which I agreed. For no matter how we disagree on other things on the matter of Mahatma Gandhi's method of taking suffering on himself I am at one with him. This is the center of his discovery and the most fundamental thing in his contribution to the world.

When Doctor Ambedkar with his retinue and I walked

out of the jail gate, the lady missionary who brought me in her car remarked, "I was very glad to be there when you came out of the jail with that Raja." The Raja was an outcaste! But Doctor Ambedkar looks the part of a Raja and has more intelligence than many of them put together, for he is a Ph.D. from Columbia, a D.Sc. from Britain, and a D.Sc. from Germany, the head of the Government Law College and a very well-read man. But an outcaste! How artificial the whole thing is! As we stood at the jail gate, Doctor Ambedkar remarked to me that what I had raised with Mahatma Gandhi in the form of questions he had raised in the form of positive statements. He added that he was not interested in temple-entry or untouchability, but in one thing, namely: Will the Hindus give us social equality, will they do away with caste? If not, we cannot stay within the structure of Hinduism. He then added that he was going to make Mahatma Gandhi commit himself by an open letter which was later sent to the daily press. In this letter Doctor Ambedkar said to Mahatma Gandhi: "If you tell me that you are fighting in the first trench, untouchability, but that your ultimate goal is to do away with caste, then I will be patient. But I want to know where you are coming out. In the end will you be in my camp or will you not?" It was the most serious challenge ever put to Hinduism, for in the person of Doctor Ambedkar sixty million aroused or arousable outcastes were speaking to Mahatma Gandhi, the representative of Hinduism. It was a very crucial moment for Hinduism. Mahatma Gandhi gave this astonishing reply: "If Doctor Ambedkar puts it in this way, then I will not be in his camp." He refused to advocate the eradication of caste. It was a reply that deeply disappointed many of his friends and gave point to my contention that, having chosen Hinduism, he has encased himself in a system from which he cannot lead the rest of us.

Hinduism gave its answer, little knowing how crucial that answer was. For later Doctor Ambedkar made his public statement before ten thousand outcastes that though he was born a Hindu he would not die one, and that he was leaving Hinduism with as many of the untouchables as would follow him. The revolt of the outcastes was in full tide and Mahatma Gandhi's reply was the swinging of the lever that opened the gates. Later he tried to stop this stampede by an article in *The Harijan* entitled, "Caste must go," but it was too late; the revolt was on. Was he too sensitive to the feelings of his Brahmin followers to come out at the crucial moment? At any rate, when he did come out, it was too late. Not that he will not hold many within Hinduism, but the vast mass will probably seek another spiritual home, a matter which has not yet been settled. Doctor Ambedkar's last word is that they are only in the destructive phases of the movement, breaking with Hinduism, the constructive choice must come later. Mahatma Gandhi's conservatism has cost Hinduism very dearly. But it is Hinduism's attitude, and Mahatma Gandhi is a Hindu, so he gave its answer.

There is another matter in which Mahatma Gandhi is behind many national leaders, and that is in the matter of people staying in their homes and being Christians. I raised the matter with him about fifteen years ago at his Sabarmati Ashram. I put it somewhat in this way: We have no desire to build up a separate communalism around the Christian Church. True, this has been done, so we seem to be another community like the Hindu and Moslem communities, and therefore seem to be driving another wedge into the already divided national life. Part of the blame for this is ours and part yours. Part is ours in that early missionaries segregated the converts to keep them from contamination. "A mission-compound mentality" has resulted. We now see the error of this and desire sincerely that we shall no longer be a nationally divisive force—we do not want to encourage denationalization of the Christians. But if the blame is partly ours, it is also partly yours, for you as Hindus would not allow people to stay in their homes and be frank, open, avowed followers of Christ. You put them out, and they were thrown into a Christian communalism. If you will allow them to stay in their homes and be frank, open Christians, this will not be. Will you allow them to do so? This was his answer: "There are thousands who are living the Christian life, but who have never heard of Christ. But I suppose this will not satisfy your Christian susceptibilities." "No," I replied, "it will not, for I want them to know Him and openly love Him." His reply here was very vague and unsatisfactory.

About fifteen years later I saw him and raised the same question, adding this: "The followers of Christ need not change their dress, their diet, their names—they can stand in the stream of India's culture and life and interpret Christ from that standpoint rather than stand in the stream of Western culture. If you are willing to allow them to stay in their homes without penalty or disability, then, as far as we are concerned, we are willing to see the Christian community as a separate social and political entity fade out, leaving a moral and spiritual organization, the Christian Church to contribute its power to India's uplift and redemption." He replied, "If my son should become a Christian under the circumstances you mention, and there should be no liquor or tobacco involved, then I should keep him in my home without penalty and without disability." I added, "But this is personal. Would you recommend this to India?" He replied, "I would, and if you take the position you now take, then most of the objections to Christianity would fade out of the mind of India." It was a most important statement, and after we left, the three of us (David Moses, principal of Hislop College, Nagpur; the Rev. S. Aldis, and I) went over our statements word for word and all agreed on what passed between us. I wrote up the interview the next day and published an account of it in the *Fellowship*. Five months later Mr. Mahadeo Desai, Mahatma Gandhi's right-hand man, came out in the public press with an apparently inspired correction saying that I had misrepresented the interview. I have the greatest admiration for Mahadeo Desai and look on him as one of the finest characters in India and consider him a friend. But this was too much! Five months later with hundreds of interviews intervening he undertook to correct what we had checked up on ten minutes after it was over and had written up the next day! It is quite true that I should have submitted an account of the interview to Mahatma Gandhi for his approval—I apologized for not doing so. But so sure were all three of us that it represented what passed between us that is never occurred to me that it needed corroboration. The whole purpose of Mahadeo Desai's "correction" apparently was to reassure the public, the Hindu public in particular, that Mahatma Gandhi had not changed in his opposition to conversion of any kind. This he had a right to do, for in the interview he had for the first time tacitly approved conversion. He apparently saw afterward that he had gone too far, hence the inspired "correction." Our reply was simple: We said, "Mahatma Gandhi has a right to say that he has not changed on the matter of 'conversion,' and we will accept it, but he has no right to say that Stanley Jones has misrepresented the facts and statements in the interview; for if Stanley Jones was mistaken, then we are all three mistaken, and equally so, for we are all agreed and that this is exactly what was said." And all three of us signed it and sent it to the paper where the "correction" appeared. To their credit they published it, and, to Mahadeo Desai's credit, he wrote and said this honest disagreement would not hurt our friendship. He is one of the most lovable of men.

But here again Mahatma Gandhi got himself into trouble because his real self and the Hindu framework in which he found himself were in conflict. I believe that the attitude he took in the interview represents his real attitude. It was so spontaneous, so out of the depths of his being that one felt that the real man was speaking. But in the "correction" another man was speaking— Mahatma Gandhi, the Hindu nationalist who, whatever His personal opinions were, could not allow the individual the right of "conversion," for that would be dangerous to the Hindu system. Again the man was bigger than the system he had adopted and the adoption of that system narrowed him, compromised him, and made him less great. I still accept him as great, one of the greatest men the world has produced, but constricted by a religious base that is smaller than he is. He got the basis of his spiritual life in Christianity in the South African days, and when he made his choice that he would remain a Hindu he superimposed that spiritual life upon the Hindu foundation and finds himself in constant contradictions on that account. For he himself is bigger than his base.

Outside of religion he is clear-cut and consistent. I can usually follow him when he speaks on other affairs. But when he gets to his religious base, he has to explain away and resort to ingenious interpretations to fit things together.

Other national leaders do not show this inconsistency, for they have no such inner contradiction regarding the allowing of people to stay in their homes and be Christians. Mrs. Sarojini Naidu, the poetess and nationalist, assented at once and said: "Certainly we should allow people to stay in their homes and be Christians. One's religion is as personal as his toothbrush."

Vijiragavachariar, once the head of the Hindu Mahasabha, the supreme Hindu body in India, and also once the president of the Indian National Congress, thus representing the widest range of interests, agreed with me at once when I put up to him the matter of Christians staying in their homes. I reminded him that what I was saying had wide ramifications and important results in the national life. He reaffirmed that he was with me absolutely, but he added, "We will let the Christians stay in our Hindu homes, but we won't let the Mohammedans." That was too much to ask! He was right about the matter, for the Moslem demands a communalism; the Christian does not. Christianity can put its roots in any national culture and can use those national cultures, for it is founded not on rules but on principles which can be applied in varying circumstances.

One national leader assured me that Christians staying in their homes would be the common practice in twenty-five years, that he was surprised that a system like caste which had been built up through centuries should go down so quickly.

"What you suggest about staying in their homes and being Christian I entirely agree with," said Srinivasa Shastri, one of the noblest men of India, "but you will find difficulty in two places—the conservative among the missionaries and the orthodox among the Hindus." Die-hards die hard in every land. But they do die!

Mahatma Gandhi still holds his place in the affections of the people as no other man does, but other and deeper forces are making his position insecure, particularly in the mind of youth; and not only in the mind of youth, but also in the older generation. And that in most unexpected places. A man arose in one of my meetings with the marks of a devotee of Vishnu very prominent upon his brow and surprised me by saying, "Don't you think it will be better if the idea of God can be wiped out of the mind of India?" I replied: "My brother, I don't know which to believe, the marks on your forehead or the words on your lips. One says you do believe in God and the other says you do not. Which shall I believe?" "Oh," he replied with a wave of his hand, "you can't tell these days what a man is thinking by the marks on his forehead. We are only waiting for Gandhi to play out, and then what I represent begins." When I asked him what he did represent, he replied, "Communism." Here was a man with all the marks of the old orthodoxy intact, and yet behind those marks a new Marx—Karl Marx was holding sway!

Socialism and Communism are disputing the future with Mahatma Gandhi and the school he stands for. Which way will India go? It is not yet decided, but whatever the future may decide, there is no doubt whatever of the amazing deposit which Mahatma Gandhi has left in the soul of India. One deposit is the awakening of India to the demand for self-government. I received a letter from a man of the Oorali, a jungle tribe of Travancore, a people who put their women folk up a tree during child birth, and one sentence struck me particularly, "The heavens will not open till we get Swaraj." Think of it! A dweller in the jungle saying that! Mahatma Gandhi's influence has largely done that. More than that, he has brought that undertone of desire out into open expression. Before the arrival of Mahatma Gandhi on the scene, the nationalist movement was, in large measure, underground, some of it violent in its outlook and attitudes.

At the close of a talk on spiritual matters a man casually

remarked to me that he had served a life-sentence (twenty years) in the Andaman Islands. When I asked him why, he replied, "For throwing a bomb at an English superintendent of police." As a lad of sixteen he was chosen by the Revolutionary Party of Bengal to try to get this Englishman because "he was in the know of our activities. I stood on the corner when his car came and threw the bomb, but it didn't explode, for we don't know how to make these things in India as well as you do in the West. So I was caught and sentenced." It seemed impossible that this mild-mannered man was a revolutionary, and yet there was much of this until Mahatma Gandhi came along and brought it to the surface. A member of the Secret Police, a plainclothes man, stayed in one of my aftermeetings for personal surrender to Christ. He came to spy and stayed to pray! As we walked home together he told me what he was doing and then added: "It is now comparatively easy for us, for Mahatma Gandhi has brought the whole thing up into the light of day. We simply go to the Congress headquarters and ask what the next step is going to be, and they frankly tell us, and it turns out as they tell us. They do not deceive us. It is easy now." That open, frank honesty is an amazing contribution to make to the public life of a country. And Mahatma Gandhi has made it. India today has shed her fears and is upstanding, and the little man is responsible in large measure.

But other forces are bidding for the allegiance of India, forces, more radical and thoroughgoing in their economic and social attitudes.

The revolt of Subhas Chandra Bose from Gandhian leadership and the formation of his Forward Bloc within the Congress calling for a revolutionary program is symptomatic. Pandit Triputi, M. L. A., addressing the newly formed All-India Radical Youth Conference said, "The possibilities of Gandhiism are now exhausted and we have to look elsewhere in order to devise effective methods of carrying on our fight for freedom. . . . The movement for independence would have become more powerful and effective had they followed other methods and not allowed themselves to succumb to Mr. Gandhi's fads." This is a real revolt and in the present mentality of the country will probably grow.

Whatever comes, Mahatma Gandhi's place in the remaking of history is deathless. In China I saw a shelf of eighty-one religious volumes all written in blood drawn from the tongue of a devotee. This history of India is being written in the blood of the strange little man, and it is not merely the blood of his tongue but the very blood of his heart.

I saw the colors in the tombs of the kings of Egypt still fresh and vivid after thousands of years. The color of the blood which Mahatma Gandhi has written into the history of India will be living and vivid thousands of years from now. For he will be looked back to as the man who discovered or rediscovered the moral equivalent of war, the method of taking suffering instead of giving it and of conquering by the method which mankind will take when it decides to leave the barbarities of war and come to real civilization. We shall all step up on the prostrate body of the little man, and when we pass on and he arises from the dust, we shall then see how truly tall and great he was. We are now too close to him to see his greatness.

CHAPTER VII

CLOGGED CHANNELS

THE India in which the Christian Church finds itself today is a live India. It is tingling with a new life. The fatalisms of the past are breaking up and change is in the air.

On board ship every day the barometer pointed to "Change," and when I asked the captain about the matter, he said it did so because it was out of order. But the barometer of India is constantly pointing to "Change" because it is in order. I said that change is in the air, but it is more than in the air—it is in definite proposals. "All of our customs are in the cooking pot," said a student. He meant the "melting pot," but it didn't matter; they were in the pot. Some of the proposals for change are wise and sane and long overdue, and some are irresponsible. The minister for Self-Government in the United Provinces, Mrs. Pandit, said to the writer, "Every morning my files are piled with ultimatums from students saying that if I don't do such and such things by such and such a time, such and such results will follow." Last night in my public meeting, a Hindu student asked whether we should not shift the basis of morals from codes to glands, that all morals had a physical basis and only a physical basis. This in the sacred city of Benares which is not supposed by orthodoxy to be a part of earth! This student would not only connect it with earth, but would make its morals of the earth.

Just now the toddy drawers went past me on the road going at a jog trot toward the market with the toddy vessels on their heads, hurrying to sell their product before fermentation had advanced too far. The fermentation of

143

new ideas in India is going on so fast that the older generation is trying hard to put some of them into operation to head off stronger demands. Will the fermentation finally result in the strong wine of Communism? Unless we can offer something better there is no doubt that it will. Is the Christian Church prepared with a bigger, a more adequate, a more inclusive gospel than Communism has to offer? Is it prepared for this hour?

I am reluctantly compelled to the conclusion that it is not. First of all, it is handicapped by the events of the West. There is such a wholesale surrender of the Christian viewpoint and a turning to other standards in Europe that it does not dispose India to accept what is being surrendered by others. It is not enough to say that they could not surrender what they had not really adopted, and that the present situation of open rejection is far better than outer adoption and inner rejection, that the situation is clarified and the issues brought to a head. That answer may satisfy the strong Christian, but it does not impress the non-Christian. His reply is that there must be some reason in Christianity itself for its failure to be adopted as a way of life by the West.

One who stands off can see that the reason for not taking the Christianity offered to the West was really for two reasons, and these seemingly opposite. Europe has failed to take Christianity as her way of life because Christianity was too compartmentalized. It did not make a total demand upon the total life. Men became tired of their own way and wanted something that would command them. Nazism, Fascism, and Communism make that total demand, and hence their acceptance by self-weary individuals. Christianity demanded too little—a-once-a-week allegiance in a part of their natures, the so-called spiritual part. The demand was not big enough. The other reason was the very opposite—it demanded too much. It called on human nature to deny itself without human nature seeing the results of that denial here and now in this life. In other words, it called for denial now and reward hereafter in heaven. The denial was real and obvious, the reward not so real or obvious. The other systems called for denial here and now and offered rewards here and now. And they got the response. Christianity to get response must make a totalitarian demand and must show that that demand brings forth its results—the best results—in human living here and now. When its demand is totalitarian and its demonstration is here and now, it will be listened to and followed. This was not done in a great part of Europe and hence the desertion. India is puzzled at that desertion and wonders what is wrong. The Christian movement labors under that handicap.

Moreover, the Church itself in India does not, on the whole, offer a different conception of Christianity. It passed on what it learned from the West—a compartmentalized conception, the spiritual compartmentalized from the material and the present from the future. On the whole it does not have a Kingdom-of-God conception from which it works out to all problems. It is not confronting India with the absolute of the Kingdom. The demonstrations which the Church in India gives are not an antidote for what India sees in Europe. For instance, I prayed at a public function presided over by a Hindu and did not use the name of Christ in closing my prayer and was roundly taken to task for it by the leader of a group of Christians. I had let Christ down. The next day his school was the scene of a riot in which his boys and others brought in by himself beat up passive resisters who asked that his school be closed on Independence Day. A lot of heads were broken, further poison injected into already poisoned Hindu-Moslem relationships, and it was touch-and-go as to whether it would not spread through the whole of the city and inflame it. To leave out the name of Christ from a prayer was unorthodoxy, but to leave out the spirit of Christ from a whole series of relationships was not unorthodox, and brought forth no reprimand. Orthodoxy was verbal, not vital. Extreme case? Yes, but symptomatic. An influential evangelist stood up before a college student body—a group of students who were making their choice between Christianity and Communism as the way for India's redemption, and of whom it was said that all the students of that university were potential or actual Communists—and this evangelist said to the students that the professors who smoked cigarettes or went to cinemas were unfit to teach the Bible to them. That was the issue—cigarettes and cinemas. While I believe that the waste through cigarettes and the dulling of the moral sense through questionable cinemas may be very real, yet compared to the issues confronting those students these were marginal. For these students were facing the whole question of the basis of the economic and social reconstruction—did Christianity offer any basis or did they have to turn to Communism? That question was not marginal, but central and fundamental. But the Church was fighting on marginal issues and leaving the central question untouched. Therefore, in the minds of those students, Christianity was an irrelevance. It was draining off men's thinking to marginal issues and leaving little time and attention for the central issues. Smugglers in Palestine put opium between the leaves of Bibles and hymnbooks, where inspectors would not suspect it being found. Figuratively, a great deal of opium has got into the Bible and into our hymnbooks when we fasten on marginal things and call our attention away from the things that are of central relevance.

The inadequacy of some approaches may be seen from this incident during the terrible floods which inundated hundreds of villages in the United Provinces. Our Ashram workers were out helping the destitute, distributing food, attending to the sick, and rescuing the people. They met some lady missionaries in a carriage, and when they asked these ladies about their work, they were told that they had been out distributing tracts to the flood sufferers. Tracts to flood sufferers! Tracts have their place, but their place is not where people are facing floods. This type of outlook has produced the saying in South India, "If you are hungry, go to a missionary and he will give you a tract!"

The Christian Church in India has taken over, in large measure, the compartmentalisms of the West, and hence it is often confused and pushed to the side lines in this struggle. Of one Christian a Communist said, "L's religion is an eccentricity, it doesn't have any effect on his social ideas and actions." His religion is an eccentricity—eccentric, off the center. It didn't come to grips with the central facts of human society. It functioned in the marginal matters, but left the center untouched. Of much of the church life in India the same thing can be said—it is an eccentricity.

Bishop Pickett's Mass Movement studies have been able and helpful and have given guidance to the Church in many matters. It has been invaluable. But at one place he left open a possibility, a dangerous possibility, which he did not intend. He insists that the central thing from which all else springs has been worship. That where the insistence on worship has been strong, social and economic results have sprung out of this insistence. But where a conscious social emphasis has been strong, results have been meager. There is no doubt that a truth is contained in this contention, but it is a truth at a certain level of life. Among a people of low culture and education, just emerging from fears and superstitions and degradations, it is a liberating experience to worship the one God as Father. It lays the basis of deliverance from fatalism, fears and filth, and from that the upward rise begins. But beyond that low level, just to worship is an incomplete thing. It would amount to taking the first Commandment—Thou shalt love the Lord thy God, and leaving out the second— Thou shalt love thy neighbor as thyself. The Russian Church was the most worshipful place of the world, but it got caught in the first Commandment and minimized the second; became a sterile institution and had to come down, replaced by a system, Communism, that insisted on the second Commandment.

Bishop Pickett is right when he says that to begin with the second Commandment among a people of low culture is a mistake, for it leaves them without the regenerating influence of the idea of one God as Father making them children in a new Family. But to start with the first Commandment and express it as worship and largely stop there by a strong insistence upon that side of things, and fail to go on to the social meanings of the second Commandment is to render a movement sterile. If it is a mistake to begin with the second Commandment it is equally a mistake to end with the first. The worship program of Bishop Pickett has made a very great contribution, but by its continued emphasis at that point through all the stages of culture and development, it is liable to become opium. It is very liable to expect social results to come by implications of worship. But the history of Europe shows that this does not follow. We have highly developed worship along with an almost complete absence of social and economic responsibility. Bishop Pickett has discovered a truth, but it is only a half truth. The social responsibility must become part and parcel of the worship and must consciously function into definite action or the worship becomes stale and sterile. But social meanings are not, on the whole, part of our worship. Our worship still expresses individualistic attitudes. Our social concepts are not a part of our ritual in any real way.

If Bishop Pickett's Survey has brought out the significance of the first Commandment of love to God expressed in worship, another Survey must now be added to stress the significance of the second Commandment of love to man expressed in social and economic regeneration. If this second survey does not supplement and correct the first, then the first may be used in a way Bishop Pickett did not intend. For it may produce side by side vested choirs and vested interests, ministers with surplices and laymen with surpluses—both unrelated to social need.

This movement for developing worship must be accompanied by a movement to develop social justice; if not, it will end in stately churches and stale Christianity.

The attention of the Churches, particularly in South India, has been absorbed a great deal in Church union, especially between the South India United Church, the Church of India, Burma and Ceylon, and the British Methodist Church. Some of the best thought of the Church has been absorbed in these discussions since 1919. During the critical period of the last twenty years, the Church has been discussing plans and proposals for union, most of them centering around episcopacy and its validities. Everyone who sees the necessity of union cannot but be grateful that union is proposed, for the Churches simply must get together. But to spend twenty years largely discussing episcopacy and ordination validities is a doubtful use of time. Episcopacy is an important part of Church government and I believe in it, but it has absorbed and still absorbs too much of the Church's attention—all out of proportion to its worth and significance in the Kingdom of God.

A Hindu Theosophist once threw a flash of light upon

this whole matter of ordination validities, and since then I've not been able to get away from his unwitting revelation. He remarked that in Theosophy they had a line of Apostolic Succession, that their two bishops, Arundale and Leadbeater, had been ordained by a bishop of the Old Catholic Church which has a straight line of tactual succession back to the Apostles. He also said that they had found out by occult means that there was "a line of magic extending from Christ through the apostles down to the present day," that "this line of magic was passed on apart from character and existed in the office of the person concerned"; that "if one from the outside got into the line, it was broken. A woman also broke the line if she got in." (Apparently she was not a good conductor!) Let us pass over the phrase "line of magic," though one cannot help but feel that he unwittingly, but truly, described the whole conception of tactual succession—it is magic, pure and simple. But the point of his statement is in the fact that he is right in saying that Theosophy has a perfect line of Apostolic Succession, for the Theosophical Liberal Catholic Church came out of the Old Catholic Church which came out of the Roman Catholic Church in unbroken succession. The succession is clear. And yet both Bishops Leadbeater and Arundale are Hindu to the core, holding to Karma, Transmigration and to other central Hindu teachings. But they are in line of Apostolic Succession! This, I am afraid, is the *reductio ad absurdum* of the theory. But it is the natural outcome of a theory that reduces Apostolic Succession to a system of tactual mechanics instead of a succession in spirit and purpose. I know that there are many who hold Apostolic Succession not as a mechanical tactual arrangement but a continuity of spirit and purpose. With them I have only agreement. But this tactual mechanism turns the gospel into something else. I simply cannot imagine Christ, who was freeing His disciples from Jewish legalism, fastening on them another legalism. The very nature of the Gospels would be denied.

However, I am prepared to let anyone hold this tactual succession idea and act on it, and I shall not look on him as other than my Christian brother, but what I do object to is to fasten that conception in an overt or covert way into any scheme of union and try to bring us all into line with it.

I am, therefore, compelled to search for a scheme of union that will allow honest differences of opinion and practice without any reservations. If anyone wants to hold tactual Apostolic Succession, he may do so to the full, but he must not impose the theory or the fact upon us as a condition of union. For if that is done, you simply read out of the scheme vast proportions of earnest Christians who simply cannot come in under these conditions. It will, therefore, not be Church Union, but a union of some Churches. Moreover, you simply force together incompatible ideas which will break apart under the strain of the future and you will lay the foundations of future splits. For, if you jam others all into one mold, then the same forces that produced the present setting up of independent bodies around the ideas of a less mechanical interpretation of Christianity will begin all over again. And the last state will be worse than the first.

We must find some way of getting together which will include honest difference of thought and practice. I am driven to some such scheme as the Branch Unity Plan. This plan came to me full-blown one day as I walked across the veranda of a mission house in Poona, not thinking particularly about Church union. It had the sense upon it of being "given," not worked out. But the more I have thought about it, the more it has gripped me. And I will tell you why. In my Round Table Conferences, in which we invite an equal number of Christians and non-Christians to tell what religion means to them in experience, I have found after listening in for many years as to what the Christians of all denominations were saying, that when they drop down beneath the level of creed and polity to experience, there they are the most united body on earth; if they only knew it. They are united in the deepest thing in life, namely, in life itself—they share the same life in Christ. They are united at the center, in life, but are divided at the margin, in polity and ritual. The Christian Church is at once the most united and the most divided body on earth.

But the first thing to note is that the Christians are united. They do not have to seek for unity—they have it, fundamentally and really.

Second, we have discovered in our Round Table Conferences that the saints are about equally distributed among all the denominations. If you were to ask me where they are most thickly congregated, for the life of me I couldn't tell you. No denomination has a "corner" on the saints. "We must keep him from being canonized," said a Roman Catholic priest to me in regard to Sadhu Sundar Singh. For it simply would not do to have a non-Catholic saint! But all the saints are not canonized, and they are not confined to any fold. God sometimes works through the denomination, sometimes in spite of it, but never exclusively or particularly in any one of them. If that hurts our denominational pride, it may help our Christian humility! The idea that any Church is the exclusive or particular channel of God's grace is as dead as Queen Anne. Somebody has said that it is "the wisdom of life to recognize a thing as dead when it is dead." Well, the exclusive-channel-of-grace conception is dead—killed by the facts. For the fact is that the degree to which God uses a man is not determined by whether he is in any particular Church, but by how deeply he is surrendered to the will of God. When God has thus spoken in the facts, why cloud the atmosphere with endless discussions about theories? God has spoken! And in the speaking He doesn't seem to be particular about the denominational framework. And if He isn't particular, why should we be?

The second thing we have discovered is equality.

The third thing is that this inner unity of life in Christ is manifested in very diverse forms, from the ornate forms of the High Churchman to the simplicities of the Quaker and all types between.

We have, then, three facts underlying the situation—Unity, Equality, and Diversity. Any scheme of union which does not take cognizance of these three things and build on them will probably fail—and ought to fail.

Is there a possibility of finding a scheme which does embody these three things? What is known as the Branch Unity Plan seems to do so. No originality can be claimed for this plan except possibly for seeing the parallels between how large bodies in national life are unified, in, say the United States and the British Commonwealth, and how they might be unified in the Church.

There were two ways you might have approached the union of the British Commonwealth or the United States. You could make all the units of this Empire or the States drop their names, wipe out their boundaries and all be ruled from London or Washington. This would never have brought unity. And yet there are people who still dream of this happening in the Church. They dream in vain! The saner view was to let each constituent unit retain its name and have a measure of self-government, but all bound together in the central loyalty to the British Commonwealth or to the United States. This method has been workable and has brought an astonishing unity in both cases. But in both cases the Unity was in the beginning very tentative. It has grown stronger with the years. In the original draft of the United States Constitution the name is written thus: "the united States." The word "united" was in small letters and was an adjective. The States were the big thing. Today the word "United" is no longer an adjective. It is a very proper noun and getting more proper all the time! It was about twenty-five years before the Constitution could be written. In the beginning the States were afraid of any central unity: the first decision of the Supreme Court of the United States was flouted by the State of Georgia. Today that is unthinkable. The States are more and more unified, but we began along the line I have advocated: not perfect union in the beginning, but set in the direction of perfect union.

There are two ways to approach Church union—one is to try to get everyone to adopt the same polity and creed and Church government, all to sign on the dotted line. If you wait for that, you will wait for a very long time, as long as the Greek kalends. A few might be willing to do it, but the vast masses would be left out. It might be a union of some Churches, but it wouldn't be Church Union. Those who hope for this are crying for the moon.

The other way is to recognize the fact that we are one, fundamentally and basically and begin to act on it. Since we all belong to Christ we should all belong to the Church of Christ. That is what I would call it, "The Church of Christ." But since we are all in different countries, I would call it, "The Church of Christ in Britain," or "The Church of Christ in America," and so on. There would be one Church and only one—"The Church of Christ." But in this one Church I would have Branches: "The Presbyterian Branch of the Church of Christ," "The Church of England Branch of the Church of Christ,"

"The Friends Branch of the Church of Christ," and so on. The figure is that of a tree with differing Branches, all adhering in the central trunk, the Church of Christ, and the trunk in turn adhering in the root, Christ, the root of us all.

Within these Branches, there could be a large measure of local self-government. If any Branch wanted bishops, they could have them and look on them as they like, but they would not impose them on the rest as the condition of unity. I do not know what Quakers would do with bishops, nor bishops with Quakers! But I do not see how the High Churchman can do without them. Likewise, if any Branch wanted adult baptism by immersion, it could have it, but again they would not impose this as a condition of unity on the rest.

In the Bishop's House at Calcutta are rooms dedicated to certain bishops with their names over the doors: "Heber Room," "Westcott Room." When anyone on the outside asked me where I was staying I would reply, "The Bishop's House," but in reply to such a question from anyone on the inside, I would say, "Heber Room." But the point was that we were all under one roof even though we did have separate names over our doors. Today the Christian Churches are not under one roof—they meet together in Conferences and Conventions, but go back to separate home roofs. The Branch Unity plan would bring them under one roof—"The Church of Christ"—while allowing them to keep a name over their door.

On our letterheads we could have "The Church of Christ" in large letters at the top, while in the margin in small letters would be "The Lutheran Branch," etc. The next time we printed them that marginal reference might get smaller, and in time we might drop it out altogether!

Moreover, under this plan there would be the possibility of amalgamation of Branches going on after we have the central unity as an accomplished fact. If any Branches wanted to come together, they could do so; there would simply be that many fewer Branches in "The Church of Christ."

Concerning transfer of members and ministers from one Branch to another, I would allow the Branches to lay down any conditions they may desire—or no conditions. In the beginning there might be conditions imposed by some, but the whole tendency would be to break down conditions. I would leave·to·tomorrow what cannot be accomplished today.

As to the structure of "The Church of Christ," there could be in each country a "General Assembly of the Church of Christ" in which matters pertaining to the whole would be dealt with. This General Assembly would be made up of representatives pro rata from the Branches. It would have such functions as would be assigned to it. The "Provincial Assembly" would deal with more local matters. Here overlapping could be faced and local situations coordinated in the light of the fact that the Branches were now cooperative instead of competitive.

The national General Assemblies could be represented in a "World Assembly of the Church of Christ," where representatives from throughout the world could meet and speak the mind of the whole Church on the public questions of the day. Suppose such a united voice could be spoken today on the subject of this impending war, calling on Christians everywhere to unite against this drift toward catastrophe! It might be averted. Alas, we have no such organ to speak for us!

Concerning the doctrinal basis, I would make it simple —as simple as Jesus did. He said that His Church was founded on the confession that Peter made, namely, that Jesus is "the Christ, the Son of the living God." This confession is the Rock beneath us all. It is literally so, even now in our divided condition. Any Branch, then, that would make the confession that "Jesus is the Christ, the Son of the Living God," I would acknowledge as fulfilling the doctrinal requirements. That one test is simple, but profound, and is the real point at issue. It would take in practically every Church in Christendom, for there we are united, amazingly so.

If one Branch would not be willing to acknowledge themselves only as a Branch and others as Branches, then, of course, there could be no unity with them. It is essential that each Branch look on itself as a Branch and only as a Branch of the Church, and not the Church, if we are to come together. If any Church should refuse to make such an acknowledgment, then we would know where we are. In that case what such a Church wants when they talk of unity is absorption and not unity. If, therefore, any Church refuses to acknowledge others as Branches, that Church has closed its mouth on Unity and must frankly talk of absorption if it is to be honest. This plan brushes away subterfuges, brings the whole thing up to the surface and makes everybody say what they mean. I am not interested in any one Church absorbing the rest. It would impoverish the whole were it to happen, for no one Church has within it the full-rounded truth. We will have to pool our resources to approximate that.

This plan of union is honest, for it acknowledges that the divisions were caused, in large measure, by the discovery of neglected truth. It now undertakes to gather up those neglected truths into the corporate body of Christendom. And how much freer we would be to take from each other if we do not force each other to take "our truth" as a price of unity! I could take the truth I see contained in Apostolic Succession if I were free to take it, but if you make the acceptance of it as the price of unity, I would have to stand forever on the outside. For I must oppose the making of anything as essential to unity, except one thing—the confession that Jesus is the Christ, the Son of the Living God. Compel me there if you will, but at every other place I must be free.

Moreover, this plan does not clamp the future. It begins with a loose unity, but the doors are open to an ever-growing unity as we live and work together. It leaves the possibility of growth as we are guided by the Spirit of God. Any plan that tries to stop up all possibility of going astray by making everybody sign a fixed constitution will only result in having no unity (for the possibility of everyone agreeing to such a fixed thing is very remote); or, if it were accomplished, it would simply split into fresh fragments by its rigidity. But in the Branch Unity Plan, we should not be frightened of difference resulting in another denomination, for we should then simply take in the new denomination and make it another Branch. But if such a spirit prevailed, the necessity of creating another denomination would be obviated, for there would be no point in doing so.

Let it be borne in mind that this plan is not Federation—it is Union. In a Federation, the constituent elements remain intact, in Union they do not do so. In this plan there are no more Churches, there is one Church and the former denominations are Branches of the one Church. It is as much Union as the United States is a Union and not a Federation.

The fact is that the very pressure of events is driving us toward Branch Unity. It is slowly coming into being, at least the framework is being laid for it. In America we have the Federal Council of Churches of Christ in America. In the so-called mission fields we have the National Christian Councils, and now the World Council of the Churches has come into being. All these are the keels laid for the further development into Branch Unity, for the Federal Council, the National Christian Councils, and the World Council could form the executives of the Church of Christ in their respective spheres. The Federal Council could naturally and normally become the executive of the "General Assembly of the Church of Christ in America"; the National Christian Councils could do the same in the different lands, and the World Council could become the executive of the "World Assembly of the Church of Christ." The Provincial Councils could become the executives of the Provincial Assemblies of the Church of Christ in India. The framework is all being laid by the very logic of events. We are being pushed in this direction. And after trying vainly to get one polity, one type of Church government and one clamped constitution, we shall eventually have to turn to some such plan as the one outlined above. At the present time those who hope to get everyone to accept an episcopal form of government will look with askance on a proposal that recognizes the validity of other forms of Church government. Theirs is a vain hope. How can the Friends take it? or the Baptists? And how can some of the rest of us take it if it means that we are all herded into a line of so-called succession as the price of unity? I love unity, but I love truth and honesty more. I cannot accept a unity that would leave out the Friends—or any other truly Christian body. I repeat, I do not want a unity of some Churches. I want Church unity.

Moreover, this plan is in line with Apostolic usage. Canon Streeter has shown conclusively that all three types of Church polity, the Episcopalian, the Presbyterian, and the Independent, existed side by side in the first century. If they did then, why not now?

We need union desperately and have not time to run into roads with dead ends. How desperately we need it is seen from the following: Representatives from the

Ezhavas of Travancore, an intelligent, forward-looking low caste, debated for some years the relative merits of the different faiths, and after thoughtful consideration decided to adopt Christianity. It was a momentous decision, for it involved eight hundred thousand people. But a lawyer arose in the caste council where this was decided and said: "Now that you have decided to adopt Christianity, may I ask you which Christianity? If you live in this section of Travancore, you will be Church of England; if in that, you will be London Mission; if in another, you will be Mar Thoma Syrian. Now you are united as a caste, then you will be divided as denominations." That simple statement stopped the whole movement.

But our divisions not only stopped this movement, they are stopping things on a wide scale, yes, on a world scale. What moral authority on unity have we among divided nations, if we cannot get together as denominations? A divided Church has little moral authority in a divided world.

But let it be clear where the stumbling block to unity is. It is in one place and only one place: the refusal of the so-called "Catholic" bodies to recognize the validity of any ordination other than their own. The minute they are willing to acknowledge the validity of forms other than their own, there will be unity. If they insist that their form and their form alone is valid, then we shall have unity in heaven, but never on earth.

We would go further. If the so-called "Catholic" bodies are willing to acknowledge that forms of ordination other than their own are valid *within the communions having them* though not necessarily among other communions, and will be willing to have such different ordinations existing side by side in a united Church, then we can have union. They need not necessarily accept them for operation within their own communions; but if they will be willing for others to have them and will not insist that we all come to one ordination, then we can have union. If this is refused, then, as far as I am concerned, I prefer not to have union. For now our differences are honest, then our unities would be dishonest.

Said an Anglican bishop to me: "It's all very simple really. You have wandered away—come back." We have no desire to "come back" if coming back means to get back to what seems to some of us to be outgrown conceptions, such as tactual succession. Our wandering away was really an attempt to get back to Christ. Therefore we have no feeling whatever of being prodigals.

But perhaps Paul has a message to both of us when he speaks of a new way of reconciliation: "to make peace by the creation of a new Man in himself out of both parties" (Ephesians 3.15, Moffatt). The way to peace was not by a compromise, but by both parties taking a step forward, and out of both parties making a new Man. Then no one wins over the other, but both win, for they are both different from what they were—a new Man emerges.

As I search my heart to see what I will have to renounce in order for the new Man to emerge, I feel that the so-called Free Churches must give up their separatist mentality and their prejudices against so-called "Catholic" bodies. And what shall the Catholic bodies give up? That is for them to say. But as far as we are concerned, there is only one thing we are waiting for: let them give up the idea of bringing us all into a line of tactual succession, let them acknowledge the validity of orders other than episcopal as valid for the Churches where these orders are exercised, and let them consent to having these two types exist side by side in the same Church, and there will be union tomorrow. If this is not possible, then union is not possible. For the union desired would be absorption, and our divisions, bad as they are, are far better than absorption. For if any group absorbed the rest, the process of breaking up would begin all over again, since the union would not be honest. And I fear I would be among the first to break away.

The Branch Unity Plan offers the opportunity of making that acknowledgment of diversity without renouncing anything each one holds as essential. It is, therefore, the acid test.

This plan would allow the possibility of producing a truly indigenous type of Indian Church, for it would not clamp the whole Church into a fixed constitution, more or less on Western lines, thus precluding the possibility of experimentation in indigenous forms. This would make room for such experimentation.

Would we exclude the Roman Catholics? We would exclude no one who would acknowledge themselves as a Branch and others as Branches. If the Roman Catholics would refuse to do this, then it is not we who close the door. It is always open. A Roman Catholic priest wrote me thanking me for my books. In reply I ended by saying: "I do wish we could feel that we are one. I have that yearning every time I pass a Catholic Church." To which he replied, "I suppose we Catholics could begin by recognizing you Protestants as Christians." I replied, "And we will reciprocate and recognize you Roman Catholics as Christians." I would gladly and joyously enter a union with the Roman Catholics on the basis that they are a Branch and we are Branches. On that basis, I could learn much from them and could appropriate every good they have. But if the union is on the basis of bringing us all under the Pope into a so-called line—never!

To recognize each other as Branches does not mean that we approve of everything in those Branches, just as to recognize a man as a fellow citizen does not mean that you necessarily approve of everything done in his home.

In the Branch Unity Plan we approve of one thing and one thing only in each other, namely, that we each confess that Jesus is the Christ, the Son of the Living God. The Rock of that confession is beneath us all. Let that suffice.

The objection is brought that this plan would not bring intercommunion and interchange of ministers. My reply is that probably nine tenths of the Protestant denominations would give intercommunion and interchange of ministers at once if Branch Union were adopted. Is that not something? Is it not far beyond anything in the way of intercommunion and interchange than could be hoped for in any plan in which all adopt the same form of Church government? Is there any hope that nine tenths would agree to such a uniform Church government union within any reasonable time? To ask the question is to answer it. Moreover, if, in the Branch Unity Plan, we began with the nine tenths straight off, we could leave to time and the Spirit of God the question of the hesitant one tenth breaking down the remaining barriers. In the meantime that remaining one tenth is within the union, subject to all the pressure of intimate contact and fellowship. Would these last two barriers not go down in time? If not, then you would have nine tenths intercommunion and interchange of ministers plus one half union of the remaining one tenth with the possibility of that remaining one half non-participation coming into full unity. It seems to me that this is a greater possibility than is offered by any other plan. And it could be put into operation at once without years of discussion. Behind all this, you have the solid fact that in the United States and the British Commonwealth these general ideas have worked in bringing together diverse portions of mankind into a living unity.

Christians of the world, unite! You have nothing to lose except your dividing walls.

The Christian movement in India looked forward to the Madras Conference for release from the clogged channels of its life. It received much help in the internal arrangements of the life of the Church. For there the Conference was at home. It knew its ground at that place. Moreover, it gave us the sense of solidarity of East and West, of the younger Churches and the older Churches; it gave us the vital leadership of the younger Churches— they assumed a decisive rôle, very often; it gave us an added emphasis upon the redeeming grace of God in Christ. But in the end it arose with no compelling vision. The reason was not hard to find.

The Conference met at a strategic moment when India was fishing about for a basis for the reconstruction of her life. Gandhiji was calling India to the simplicities of India's past, and Jawahar Lal was calling India to take hold of the complexities of the present and socialize the means of production and distribution in order to produce a juster distribution of economic goods, this to be done apart from religion. The farseeing recognize that what is needed is Gandhiji's spirit of religion with Jawahar Lal's insight into economic reconstruction. The tension between them is great, but both groups are being held together by the burning spirit of nationalism. A synthesis of these viewpoints had not yet been attained. The time was ripe for the Christian movement to step into the situation with a message and program which would have made that synthesis—plus something lacking in each. Obviously, the Kingdom of God was the conception that thoughtful men were looking for, although perhaps unconsciously. The individualistic interpretation of religion was insufficient, and the only social application of it that India knew was communalism. The latter turned youth away from religion in disgust, for it was dividing the country. Communistic thought was growing by leaps and bounds, mostly under the banner of Socialism for the Communist party as such is illegal. We needed something that would lift the whole of religion onto a new plane of thought and action. The whole situation was looking for a word, a master-word which would become a master-conception. That word was "the Kingdom of God."

The Madras Conference could have spoken that word. But it did not do it. And it has left us not much beyond where we were. It did not give into the hands of the Church a master-key, so the Church is still fumbling with all kinds of keys, ranging all the way from a narrow individualistic salvation to a Humanistic Socialism, and everything between. Nothing to gather up life into an integrated, meaningful whole. Outside the Church, the most religious race on earth is turning from religion to irreligious Socialism or Communism, for it does not see the possibility of putting the whole of life together on a religious basis. Some few are presenting to India and to the Christian Church that master key, the Kingdom of God, but India looks on them as an eccentricity, out of the stream of Church life as it were, not representing the whole Christian movement. They cannot complain that India does not listen to them, nor that she does not appreciate the message—she does, but India is able to dismiss it more easily with the thought that this represents a few individuals and is not what the Christian movement as a whole stands committed to. Madras could have committed the whole Christian movement and could have thrown this issue into the center of India's life and thought as the supreme issue. But it did not. Why?

The background of the thinking of the Madras Conference was Doctor Kraemer's able book. In season and out of season the book insists that we must not be caught in relativisms, we must confront the world with an absolute.

That absolute was the Absolute God. He interprets Himself through Jesus Christ. So far, so good. I agree. But here a jump was made in the thought of the Conference. From the Absolute, God, they jumped to the Church as the working thought of the Conference. But the Church is a relativism. "The Church is not the absolute which we seek in order to escape from relativity" (*Revelation and Response,* Dickie, page 134). At its best, the Church by its very nature is a relativism. If you say you think of the invisible Church, the body of saints being perfected as the Church and not this outer organization, then the answer is the same. That too is a relativism. This body of saints is in a state of being perfected; it is, therefore, not absolute and what is not absolute is a relativism. The Conference was thus compelled to work from one relativism to other relativisms. Hence its voice was weak. The Conference confronted the relativisms of Race as in Nazism, State as in Fascism, Class as in Communism with another relativism, the Religious Community, the Church. All of these are relativisms, and hence none of them the hope of the world. But the Madras Conference put forth the Church as the hope of the world: "The Church is, under God, the hope of the world." This sentence, contained in "The Message," was no chance statement. It summed up the presuppositions of the Conference. If the Church was the working concept of the Conference, then it had to be put forth as the hope of the world. There was nothing else to be put forth. The Conference was thus betrayed by its premises into putting forth one relativism to match and replace the other relativisms of Race, State, and Class. So the Madras Conference, at the very time it was warning us, through Doctor Kraemer, against falling into relativisms, fell into the very thing it was warning us against. Hence its inability to give a clear lead on many things.

Had it worked down from the Absolute of the Kingdom of God to the relativisms of Church, Race, State, Class, Family and Individual, it would have had a clear incisive lead to give, for all of these would have taken their place under the Absolute.

That was the place Jesus started from: "He went out preaching the gospel of the Kingdom of God." The Kingdom of God was the gospel. It is the only thing He ever called the gospel. Paul called it by other names: "the gospel of the grace of God," "the gospel of Christ," but Christ Himself called one thing and one thing alone the gospel—the Kingdom of God. There are those who would break the force of this by saying that the gospel or good news was the near coming of the Kingdom—the gospel was not the Kingdom, but the nearness of its coming. This is a mistake, for remote or near the Kingdom of God is the good news. It is that for which we are made, therefore it is the good news.

Mark, in the opening verse of his life of Christ, speaks of "the beginning of the gospel of Jesus Christ." Was the gospel of Jesus Christ the gospel He brought, namely, the Kingdom of God, or was He, Himself, the gospel? There we get the key to the whole thing: it was both. And it had to be both.

The Kingdom of God seems to be a new Order, God's Order confronting the lower order. This higher Order, founded on redemption of the sinful and the weak, brotherhood, mutual aid, and love, confronts the lower order founded on selfishness, unbrotherliness, mutual elimination. This higher Order is offered to the individual and the collective will: "the Kingdom of God shall be taken away from you and given to a nation bringing forth the fruits thereof." The nation, as well as the individual, was to embody this Order.

This was His message. But He seemed later to shift

the emphasis to Himself: "I am the Way," "Come unto me, and I will give you rest." Why? Well, this sequence was necessary. He had to lay the foundation of the new Order in their thinking, and then He had to present Himself as the embodiment of that new Order, the new Order personalized.

The leader-principle can only be operative as the leader embodies a Cause. Hitler could not lead Germans unless he embodied Germany as it were, the symbol of Germanism. Mussolini embodies the new aggressive Italy; Lincoln embodied democracy for everyone, white and black; devotion to Gandhi is devotion to Indian nationalism. No leader can lead unless personal loyalty to him is loyalty to a Cause embodied in him. If he only represents a person, he will lack contagion. A few will gather around him, but only a few. The masses must see in him the embodiment of their hopes and longings, their Cause.

Jesus, therefore, did not appear as an individual—He appeared as the embodiment of the Cause of Causes, the Kingdom of God. It was the one thing for which all mankind is consciously or unconsciously longing: an all-inclusive Order which shall gather up into itself the lesser meanings and loyalties of life and give coherence and purpose to the whole. Nothing less than a Universal Order can do this. The only Universal Order is the Kingdom of God.

But only a Universal Person can embody a Universal Order. Only the Son of man can embody the hopes and longings of the sons of men. Christ as the Son of man, the Universal Man, embodied in Himself the Universal Order, the Kingdom of God. The Universal Person and the Universal Cause met and were one.

Jesus was the Key to that Kingdom. Just as Jesus reveals the nature of God, He reveals the nature of the reign of God. The Kingdom of God is Christlikeness universalized. God reigns in the spirit that Jesus reigns, and with the same weapons of coercion, the coercion of the Cross. This is important, for many still conceive of God beating down His enemies by force and establishing His reign. If Jesus is kept as the Key, then this force-conception of the Kingdom fades out and the Cross, as the working force, becomes dominant. Gandhi touched a long-lost chord and thrilled the world by giving us a glimpse—only a glimpse, but a real glimpse—of this power of taking suffering instead of giving it and applying it on a national scale. He awakened within us the thought of the Kingdom and its weapons—and we were startled at how far we had strayed and of how far we could go if we rediscovered the Kingdom and its weapons.

This, then, was the gospel: God's absolute Order embodied in an absolute Person confronts us with its redemptive offer and demand. It is not an impersonal Order confronting us, but an Order that looks out from tender eyes—the Order is warm and human.

The Madras Conference, with no real grip of the Kingdom, preached a warm and human Christ, but with no Kingdom embodied in Him. Hence the Christ thus preached lacked significance for the total life. It tried to make the Church the working conception from which it worked out to its problems. When you do that, you are soon floundering, for you are working from one relativism to other relativisms. The result—confusion. But when you work from the Absolute Kingdom to the relativisms of Church, Race, State, Class, Family, and Individual, you cut straight through everything with a sure word. All of these get their significance from something higher than itself—the Kingdom of God. They have their meaning in relationship to something higher, hence they are relativisms. The Kingdom of God is not related to something higher than itself—it is the Absolute.

When the Madras Conference sent its message to the world it said, "Madras discovers the Church." It did discover the world-wide ecumenical body. As such, it was a splendid discovery. But it was not a big enough discovery, not for this hour—or any hour. It was like discovering a lake when you needed an ocean. What was needed was an all-embracing conception that was truly totalitarian to face all the lesser so-called totalitarians with a pre-emptory demand: Submit.

The Church cannot say that. Not of itself. Only one Church tries it—Rome. In the Roman conception, the Kingdom of God and the Church are one. This we cannot accept. Suppose we go out saying, "Repent, for the Church is at hand." People would laugh, as an audience actually did when I said it. But people do not laugh when you say, "Repent, for the Kingdom of God is at hand," for they feel instinctively that they are confronted with an Absolute. The Church is a means, the Kingdom of God is the end. The Church is temporary, the Kingdom of God is permanent and eternal. There is no Church in heaven, there is nothing else but the Kingdom of God in heaven. The Kingdom of God is wider than the Church. The Church is the best means, but not the only means of the Kingdom of God. The Kingdom lays hold on movements outside of the organized Church: Gandhi in India showing us the way of the Cross in public life; the scientific movement in its passion for truth and the service of man; the brotherhood movements that demand social justice, and so on. They are a part of the Kingdom movement to the degree that they embody the Kingdom ideas and spirit. I am not satisfied with the degree they manifest. I cannot be satisfied with any movement or person until he humbly bows and receives the grace of God in Christ. But this does not preclude my being grateful that God is using movements and persons even before they bow in conscious obedience to Christ. God said to Cyrus: "I have called thee though thou hast not known me." He is doing the same today.

The Church, being relative, must come under the judgment and correction of something higher than itself—the Kingdom of God. Only as it loses its life in obedience to this higher Order does it find its life coming back to itself. It has authority only as it submits to and embodies this higher authority. But if, by emphasis, it saves its life, it loses its life; it degenerates into an ecclesiasticism with its lofty pretensions and little moral authority.

The Church very, very often does become an end in itself—it demands that it be served, one is supposed to be good as he attends it, contributes to it, upholds it. When this attitude is taken, the Church, for all practical purposes, is an end. But when the Church is looked on as a means to the ends of the Kingdom of God, the whole mentality changes. Everything is directed beyond itself to Kingdom ends. A breath of cleansing higher authority goes through it, cleansing away the mustiness of corporate self-centeredness. The authority of the Church is judged by one thing—and one thing alone—how much does it serve? For it is the same for the individual and the corporate group—the greatest among them becomes the servant of all—greatness in authority comes as a result of dedication to ends beyond itself.

The Church at Madras came desperately near to saving its life by emphasis and of thereby losing itself. The fact is that it did lose authority in the contemporary situation by its very lack of a comprehensive totalitarian message. The newspapers of India passed it by as of little significance. Its emphasis on itself was more or less in line with all the rest of the religious communalisms of India which were a stench in the nostrils of right-thinking Indians.

Had this Conference come with a Kingdom emphasis

which would have lifted the whole of religion out of communal antagonisms and would have confronted India and the Church with God's Order, it would have become the immediate issue of all India. But in all my subsequent meetings for months across India immediately afterward, I was not asked a single question at Question Time about the Madras Conference. It raised no compelling issues.

When the Conference came to the question of declaring itself on the two burning issues of religious persecution and national aggression, the best it could do was to issue a statement as to why it could say nothing, the reason for the silence being that any pronouncement would upset our fellowship—the Germans and the Japanese would be offended. The end was to hold the fellowship.

That was not a chance conclusion, it was the working out of the very basis of the Conference. If the working conception of the Conference is the Church, then the great end is to preserve the Church fellowship on no matter how low a basis. This was done. No pronouncement was made. The fellowship was saved. But at what a cost! We renounced our moral leadership to save our fellowship.

If we had only begun with the Kingdom, as Jesus did! When I said that, a missionary replied that Jesus had to begin with the Kingdom for the Church was not yet in being. In other words, the Kingdom was an interim idea brought in until the Church came into being—a complete misunderstanding of the gospel. The Kingdom was no interim idea brought in until the Church was formed, but it was the master-conception with which the gospel begins and ends. The Church was in being when two disciples followed Christ, but the Kingdom conception did not thereby fade out and the Church conception take its place. The thing that Jesus discussed for forty days after the resurrection was "the Kingdom of God" (Acts

1. 3). The very last verse in Acts says that Paul preached "the kingdom of God." And the disciples still preached it as the gospel of "the Kingdom of God" (Acts 8. 12). It was their gospel as it had been Christ's gospel. Obviously, it was no interim idea brought in till the Church came into being, but was the master-conception which contained every lesser thing within itself including the Church.

When I said the disciples preached the Kingdom of God as their gospel it must be modified a bit. There were two centers to their gospel—two centers which became one. Just as Jesus went out preaching the gospel of the Kingdom of God and the gospel of Himself as the embodiment of that Kingdom, so the disciples preached those same two things: they preached the "good news of the Kingdom of God and the name of Jesus" (Acts 8. 12, Goodspeed). And "he [Paul] preached the Reign of God and taught about the Lord Jesus Christ" (Acts 28. 31, Moffatt). These two things were really one—they were the alternate beats of a single heart. The Absolute Order and the Absolute Person had come together and formed a single gospel.

This was not the gospel of the Madras Conference. It proclaimed the Absolute God through Doctor Kraemer, Jesus Christ as the bridge between the Absolute God and man, and the Church as the resultant of this redemptive impact. The Kingdom of God, as the link between the Absolute God and all relativisms, was scarcely mentioned except as a flourish at the end of a few sentences. It is true, that after my criticism of the Conference at this point, the secretaries after the close of the Conference sprinkled in the phrase, "the Kingdom of God," here and there in the Reports, but in the original draft of "The Faith by which the Church Lives," there was not even a paragraph on the Kingdom. It was not the working conception of the Conference. The Church was. They worked out all problems from the standpoint of the Church. In other words, they worked from one relativism to other relativisms. The result—confusion and hesitation.

When attention was called to the fact that Jesus used the phrase "the Kingdom of God" sixty-four times (altogether a hundred times, if parallel accounts are included) and "the Church" twice (and both times in only one Gospel), but the Report on "The Faith" had reversed this and had used "the Kingdom" twice (three times, to be accurate), the Report was sent back and "the Kingdom of God" was put into a paragraph—into a paragraph, and that as an afterthought! That was symbolical—the Kingdom of God was an afterthought put into a paragraph. It was not the working conception of the Conference.

Exactly the same thing happened in this Conference as apparently happened in the Conferences drawing up the creeds of Christendom in the early Christian centuries. Do they embody the Kingdom of God as the working conception as Jesus did? Call the roll and see. The so-called Apostles' Creed does not mention it, nor does the Athanasian Creed. The Nicene Creed mentions it once, but after the resurrection, a future heavenly Kingdom—"Thy Kingdom is an everlasting Kingdom." The master-conception which Jesus mentioned a hundred times they mention once, but that once was not a working conception now on earth. It was future and heavenly. A cog had been slipped. A supreme lapse had taken place. I hesitate to call it the Great Betrayal, and yet it is dangerously near to being just that. For with the conception of the Kingdom left out, the creeds had no social message —no conception that brought the whole of life, individual and social, under a single control. An individualistic and other-worldly conception of Christianity went across the Western world—a crippled Christianity leaving a crippled result. Christianity was to function in the inner life now, and in the whole of the life only beyond the borders of this life in heaven. Whole areas of life now were left out of its control and turned over to Mammon. A compromise was entered into with Mammon—it would rule the economic and consequently the social, the political, and the international, while Christianity would take the area of the inner life as its sphere on earth, and in heaven by and by it could take over the whole of life. That has been the practical working agreement entered into—Christianity would be tolerated if it stayed in its place. And the conception of Christianity given to us in the Creeds allows that to be done. That is the dualism running straight through Western civilization, a dualism making for hypocrisy and strain. This dualism was ended by three modern movements. Communism attempts to end it, taking over the whole of life under the single conception of Marxian, scientific materialism. It is totalitarian. Fascism ends it by taking everything over in the name of the State: "Nothing above the State, nothing outside the State, nothing against the State, everything within the State." It is totalitarian. Nazism ends it by taking everything over in the name of Race. It too is totalitarian.

Into the vacuum created by the abdication of Christianity from the economic and social, has rushed these totalitarian movements to take over what we had refused to take over. Please do not answer that the Church did take over the whole of life during the Middle Ages—and with what result! The answer is simple: The Church attempted to take over the whole of life, but it meant that one relativism attempted to take over other relativisms. In doing so, the Church was bound to arrogate to itself an absolutism and an infallibility. This broke down and with it the scheme built up on it. The Church could not sustain the task of taking over the whole of life. It was bound to fail and should fail.

These other relativisms of Class and Race and State will have their day and break down as they try to take the rôle of the Absolute and control the whole of life. For the time being, men will hail them as the saviors from unsatisfying dualisms and will feel the thrill of something apparently absolute—and then the disillusionments and the breakdown. Men are made for the Absolute Order, but the Absolute Order is not the Church, or Class or Race, or State. That Absolute Order is the Kingdom of God. That is the Order men are unconsciously feeling for through Church and Class and Race and State. They want something to command them absolutely and in that commanding of them to give them their freedom.

The Madras Conference, representing the front line advance of Christendom, should have seen this more clearly than those who are the home base. For in the missionary advance the issues are laid bare more quickly and surely. All irrelevancies have to be stripped away as we advance into the soul of the human race. But Madras did not see it, for Madras was the offspring of Oxford and Edinburgh and continued the Church-centric thought of these two Conferences.

Some of the members of the younger Churches were ripe for a new beginning—witness the Chinese and Indian delegations—but the Conference had been started out on a Church-centric groove and could not get out of it. The younger members were powerless to make a fresh beginning even if they had seen the issues clearly. One South American delegate said after the Kingdom Absolute was presented: "I knew there was something wrong with the Conference, but I didn't know just what it was. It is all clear now."

When the attention of the Conference was called to this lack of Kingdom emphasis in the Message, the reply was given by one of the drafters of that report, "The Kingdom conception is so difficult to define that we could not use it." The one thing Jesus talked about most is so difficult to grasp and define that is it unusable! Here was a solar plexus blow to the Christian gospel, and when it was uttered no one winked an eye. At least no voice was raised in protest. Apparently, we had become used to doing without the Kingdom as the master-conception and did not miss it, nor did we consider it heresy when we were told it could not be used. Today I read, "Smite the shepherd, and the sheep shall be scattered." Smite the shepherd of our souls by saying His central idea and working conception is unusable, and in deed and in truth the sheep are scattered. We are not only scattered, we are done for. For we have pinned our hopes completely on this Man and His Kingdom. But if His Kingdom is unusable, I wonder about the Man Himself. Is He usable? Perhaps as a King without a Kingdom. But the moment I say it I am inwardly collapsed—who wants a King without a Kingdom?

The Continental brethren in a separate pronouncement brought in the Kingdom, but as entirely future and apocalyptic. Their conception of the Kingdom was not usable —now. While there is a set of teachings of Christ that definitely make the Kingdom future and apocalyptic, there is just as definite a set of passages that teach that the Kingdom comes by a gradualism here and now: "The Kingdom of heaven is like a grain of mustard seed which grows into a great tree" (the outward growth); "The Kingdom of God is like unto leaven . . . until the whole is leavened" (the inner permeative growth). There are those who, embarrassed by this gradualism, explain it away by saying that leaven is always used as a symbol of evil. But is "the Kingdom of God like unto evil"? To ask it is to answer it. No; there are two sets of passages very clearly given in the New Testament—one teaches a gradualism and the other an apocalypticism and both are legitimate parts of the account and neither can be taken out without disrupting the account. We need both. For the gradualism gives me my task here and now, and the apocalyptic gives me my hope—my hope that the last word in human affairs will be spoken by God perhaps suddenly and that last word be "victory." The Kingdom, then, is something both present and future; we work for it and we wait for it.

We work for it. We can become the agents and instruments of its coming. I cannot understand the statement of Doctor Kraemer when he says in his book, which was the basis of the Conference: "The Kingdom is not the object of our striving or our achievement; it is in the Father's hands." That sounds like fatalism. It is true that the Kingdom of God cannot be "built" as we often say in such phrases as "building the Kingdom," for it smacks too much of a Humanism. The Kingdom is "received." "It is the Father's good pleasure to give you the kingdom" —it is the gift of God. But all the parables of growth and the leaven involve man's activity and cooperation, the seed is sown, watered, the field is weeded and attended to; the woman took the leaven and placed it in the meal. Man cooperates with God. The sentence of Doctor Kraemer might just as easily read: "The Kingdom is not the object of God's striving or His achievement; it is in our hands." In both cases it would be a half-truth, and therefore by itself wholly false. The Kingdom is God's Kingdom, but God does not rule over us except with our consent and cooperation. The Kingdom, therefore, is in the hands of both God and man. We work for it and we wait for it.

When I insist on primary Kingdom emphasis, am I disloyal to the Church, as someone has suggested? I plead not guilty. The Church is the mother of my spirit, and without her I could not have survived as a Christian. The best life of the Kingdom is contained in the Church. But I know the limitations of even my mother. Where we make a relative thing into an absolute thing there is idolatry. The Church is relative, and to make it take the place of the Kingdom of God is dangerously near to idolatry. I can be, and am, loyal to my fingertips to a Church which is loyal to the Kingdom of God, which comes under the judgment of the Kingdom, is the instrument and servant of the Kingdom, and which embodies the spirit and life of the Kingdom. But I am disloyal to a Church which is disloyal to the Kingdom by becoming an end in itself.

It has not been easy to make this criticism of the Madras Conference, for the men and women I admire most in the world were there. For weeks I smothered it within my heart, and then I found myself untrue to a life principle we have adopted in the Ashram: No inward secret criticism. But in expressing the criticism, I knew it was like launching a torpedo at the very heart of the Conference. There would be obvious resentment on the part of those responsible. I have bowed my head for the return blow. To my surprise I found an astonishing amount of agreement. Even one Lutheran bishop who was chairman on the section of the Church said: "If I had heard you before I wrote the report on the Church, it would have been a very different report. You have converted me to the Kingdom. And to convert a Lutheran is no easy task." There has been an astonishing agreement. But of course there has been resentment.

I care for this missionary enterprise so desperately that I am willing to take the brunt of it, knowing that the years will bear me out. This Church emphasis of the Conference will run out and show its inadequacy in a few years, and then we shall have to have another conference to rediscover the Kingdom. When we do, then we shall rehabilitate the total missionary enterprise, perhaps the total Christian movement.

For the whole Christian movement stands confused before a world situation which is breaking down. It has no master-concept to match against this hour. As a result of compartmentalizing its life, it has no totalitarian demand to make upon the life of the race. Hence, other totalitarianisms rush into this vacuum and hold the areas of life which Christianity did not control. The only hope for the rehabilitation of Christianity is to get back a totalitarianism which will control the whole of life. Experiments are being made to get back to a totalitarianism, and to one such experiment we now turn.

CHAPTER VIII

THE ASHRAM MOVEMENT

THE Christian Ashram movement is an almost spontaneous movement within the Church in India. It did not come into being as an official product of the Church, it has simply arisen from within the movement itself to answer a need. It is true that the Madras Conference put its stamp of approval upon it when it suggested that new missionaries should stay some months or a longer period in Ashrams to get training before beginning their missionary career. In a way this puts the Ashram movement within the stream of Christian orthodox practice. But the approval was largely on the basis that it brought the missionary closer to the soul of India through this indigenous form of life. But the Christian Ashram movement is a far deeper searching for ultimate answers than just providing a more indigenous expression of Christianity. It does desire to provide an indigenous expression, but more—it is really an attempt, perhaps half-unconsciously, to put a totalitarianism back into life. It has arisen spontaneously in varying types to meet that need. There are now about twenty-four Christian Ashrams in India, most of them having sprung up in the last few years.

The derivation of the word "Ashram" is variously given. Some authorities say it is from *a*—from, and *shram*—hard work: a cessation from hard work. Others say the *a* is intensive, and that the word means an intensification of hard work. The fact is that both kinds of manifestation of the Ashram spirit can be found. Some go aside from life and toil and go into Ashrams to get quiet so as to give themselves to a life of meditation and realization of God. It is a cessation of hard work. On the other hand,

181

there are types that go into Ashrams for a mental and spiritual discipline in order to give themselves to the service of the outside world. Far from being a cessation of hard work, it is an intensification of it, for the hard work is both upon oneself in discipline and upon others in service, often of the most menial kind. Between these two outstanding types there are many variations.

For let it be understood that there is no orthodox type of Ashram, either in Hinduism or in the Christian expression of it. Mahatma Gandhi's Ashram at Sabarmati revolved around the idea of national service, largely through indigenous cottage industries. The intellectual content was not emphasized. It was religion trying to rehabilitate the country. On the other hand, Rabindranath Tagore's Ashram revolves around culture, art, and poetry with an agricultural appendage. The more orthodox types give themselves to religious meditation and corporate spiritual quest. There is no standardized type of Ashram. When some Christians questioned whether the Sat Tal Ashram could legitimately be called an Ashram, some Hindus took up the matter and issued a statement saying that our Ashram could be legitimately called an Ashram.

The Ashram really springs from the ancient forest schools, where a guru, or teacher, would go aside with his chelas, or disciples, and in corporate spiritual quest would search for God through philosophical thought and spiritual exercises. But let not the Western reader think that he has caught the idea when he labels the Ashram a monastery or hermitage. It has some of the characteristics both of the monastery and hermitage and yet it has its own distinct Indian flavor which makes it different from both. It is the national soul of India expressing itself in religion, the central characteristic of which would be simplicity of life and an intense spiritual quest. The Ashram began in the forest, but many Ashrams were and are in the heart of cities.

The spiritual quest through the Ashram form has gone along three lines—the Gyana Marga, the way of knowledge; the Bhakti Marga, the way of devotion; and the Karma Marga, the way of works. They correspond to the modern division of the personality into intellect, feeling, and will. But we cannot separate our quests in this way, for obviously we need something to gather all three into one Way. For life cannot be compartmentalized. It must be a living whole. We feel that in Christ all three ways are gathered into one, for He is the Way—a method of acting, the Karma Marga; the Truth—the way of knowledge, the Gyana Marga; the Life—the way of devotion, the Bhakti Marga.

It was natural, therefore, to look on Christ as the fulfillment of the Ashram spirit which had within it all three ways of expression. It was also natural for the Christians to lay hold on the Ashram form of expression and make it their own, for the Ashram had little or no associations with idolatry; it fitted in with the Christian idea of simplicity and corporate spiritual quest. It seemed to be the very thing the Christians were looking for, for in this indigenous mold the Indian Christian would be at home, he would be on his own ground, could think his own thoughts and be creative.

The Western denominational molds have left him largely dissatisfied. The Church is for the most part a worshiping institution used once or twice a week. This makes the fellowship a momentary thing of an hour or two in seven days. After those few hours, each goes back into his compartmentalized life. The Indian mind—in fact, the human mind—wants something that will gather the whole of life into a central control and make it into a fellowship which will not be for an hour or two, but something continuous and all-embracing. The Protestant forms of religious denominationalism grew up during the time of the sway of individualism. They are the outer expression of that individualism—a man's corporate life is largely unchanged by it: he stays in his separate family life, carries on his business in his own way, has his chosen club relationships, goes to church on Sunday to listen to exhortations to do certain things largely as individuals. Now and again there is corporate action, but, on the whole, the Christian Church in its ordinary form fits into an individualistic scheme of thought and life. This has its advantages and has made a wonderful contribution. It has made for strong, aggressive individuals. These strong Protestant individuals in a capitalistic order rose to the top in accumulation. They were frugal and moral according to the morality of individualism. But all this has run its course and has shown its shortcomings. We see that life is corporate as well as individual. The pendulum swings from individualism to the various types of Socialism—national, communistic, and other brands. The dialectic is at work. The thesis of individualism produces the antithesis of Communism and national Socialism. We look forward to that synthesis, the Kingdom-of-God order, which will gather up into itself all the good of individualism and Socialism and fulfill each and add something lacking in each.

It was this quest for a Kingdom-of-God order that drove some of us to adopt the Ashram as a possible mold in which this order might be expressed. This quest for the Kingdom-of-God order was not primary in the beginnings of the establishment of our Ashrams. That came out as we went along. For we are being driven deeper and deeper. We began in rather a surface way—surface and yet very real, and for that period a very radical departure.

We began the Sat Tal Ashram ten years ago much as

Abraham did when "he went out not knowing whither he went." We felt the urge and started. We saw certain necessities before us. In the political realm the Gandhi movement for self-government was in full swing. It was obvious that the Christian movement had to live in an India that would be self-determining. No matter how many progressive stages along the way the end was obvious. And the national movement was more than a political movement—it was deeply religious and cultural. It is now becoming economic as well. How could the Christian movement exist if it were looked on as the religious side of the foreign domination? It must disentangle itself from that foreign domination and identify itself with the stream of India's life and aspiration. Otherwise, if it is identified with the foreign domination, it will decay with the decay of that domination. The Ashram seemed to offer the mold for that identification with India. It was religious, it was cultural, it was economic, it was nationalistic. So we took it.

Besides, we also saw that with the decay of Western domination in India and the rise of the Indian to a place of self-determination in his own land, the relationship of the foreign missionary and the indigenous worker would have to change. If they worked together for the future, the relationship could no longer be master and servant. It had largely become this, not from desire entirely, but from the fact that the missionary usually held the purse strings. And he who pays the piper calls the tune. The missionary, his standard and ways of life, was calling the tune. Each worker wanted to rise to the status of the missionary, occupy his bungalow and have his authority. That was all natural under the circumstances. In the Anti-Religious Museum in Moscow I saw, as one of the exhibits, a large and splendid two-storied missionary bungalow alongside of an African native hut. This, they said, is how religion works out its equality. That picture stung. But how to bridge these two? Two standards of life had come together in India. Many of the foreign missionaries came from America, the richest country in the world. To raise the Indian to the economic standards of the missionary would mean to get him all out of touch with his social environment and create a gulf between him and his people. Besides, it was economically impossible. On the other hand, for the missionary to try to come to the physical level of India would mean to court physical breakdown. Some had tried it with disastrous results. Some form of life was needed where the Indian standard would be "raised" and the missionary standard "lowered."

The Ashram seemed to provide that form. There the Indian and the foreigner could meet on an economic and cultural basis which would be close to the Indian standards of simplicity and, at the same time, provide a sufficiently healthful basis for the foreigner. For the corporate life could be organized on a scientific basis as to food values and sanitation. The Ashram has, therefore, stepped into a transitional period and has provided a basis on which East and West can get along together under these changed circumstances.

The Ashram, therefore, could provide a place where the streams of individualism and Socialism and the streams of East and West might come together in a new full life. And all of it would center around Christ. Not that we had any such full-rounded ideas when we first began.

I suppose it began partly out of the urge to bring the Christian movement into closer relationship with nationalistic India and partly through the feeling that, as an evangelist, I needed to demonstrate in some concrete way, through an institution, the things I was talking about in public. It would give me the discipline of concreteness, the necessity of trying out one's ideas under life itself.

It is difficult to be an evangelist and a Christian. One becomes wordy, cocksure, censorious, abstract, unless he has the discipline of the necessity to demonstrate in actual concrete situations what he is talking about. Every evangelist, therefore, should be a pastor of a church, at least part time, or connected with some institution where his word would have to become flesh.

Moreover, the Christian worker needs not only the discipline of the concrete, but he also needs the discipline of a close-knit group, to which he is responsible, and where there is an understanding pledging of ourselves to each other to help the growth of each by constructive suggestions and frank criticism. For twenty-two years I had no such fellowship, and I am the poorer for it. I was telling others what to do, but no one told me. It is true that I had the Question Hour in public meetings, where criticism could be put in questions, but this criticism, while helpful, did not meet the situation, for it came not from an inner circle, but from the outside fringe. And the questioners and the questioned were not pledged to a conspiracy of mutual helpfulness. It was irresponsible.

The future of the world is in the hands of the disciplined—in the hands of those who can subordinate a present desire for a future end and who can act in a disciplined corporate way. The reason why Nazism, Fascism, and Communism have gone so far is because, for good or evil, they represent a disciplined way of life. Hence, they cut through undisciplined situations around them like a knife through cheese. This is seen vividly in disciplined Japan cutting through undisciplined China. Discipline is a power—for good or ill.

The Christian movement began in a disciplined group, a Master with His twelve disciples. They were to live in simplicity and single-mindedness and corporate loyalty— all this in order to be the individual and corporate instrument of the Kingdom of God. Christianity began as a group movement. The word "disciple" and the word "discipline" sound alike; they are alike. No discipleship without discipline.

But discipline has largely dropped out of the Protestant expression of Christianity. One can see why this has happened. We emphasized individual responsibility to God and the doctrine of grace. In teaching the doctrine of grace we said that all penances, self-disciplines, and good works were powerless to save—we were saved by the redeeming grace of God. So we let disciplines go, and in letting them go we threw out the baby with the bath. We let go discipline, individual and corporate. Salvation *is* by the grace of God, but salvation needs discipline to make it individually and corporately effective.

As a reaction to this undisciplined type of Christianity, there is growing up a number of movements, all of them attempting to put discipline back into life—the Oxford Group movement, a movement which disciplines itself under the four absolutes; Kagawa's Fellowship of the Friends of Jesus; the Christian Ashram movement. These are healthy signs, provided these movements are disciplined to the thought that they do not represent the Kingdom of God, but are only varying approximations of that Kingdom and must, themselves, come under the higher discipline of that Kingdom. Only thus can they be saved from self-righteousness and a holier-than-thou attitude, which, it may be emphasized, is a very real danger.

We began as a part-time Ashram in the Himalayas at Sat Tal. It still seems a miracle that we have this glorious estate of four hundred acres, with a lake of its own and bordering on two government lakes, its eighteen cottages and the central large house in which the Ashram is held. The altitude is five thousand feet and takes us out of the terrible summer heat. It was developed as a summer resort by a British engineer and we took it over as an adventure of faith. We began on a shoestring, but our resources have not failed. The physical plant was perfect for our purposes, for here the vacation period could be combined with a strong spiritual purpose running through it.

We felt the urge to combine the Indian spirit and the Christian spirit. The Indian spirit is difficult to define, but anyone who has come in contact with it knows what I mean—an inner poise, a spiritual sensitiveness, a love of simplicity, an emphasis on the gentler virtues, a spirit of devotion, an ascetic tinge. Just the spirit to be touched and redeemed by the Christ spirit. The adventure of putting them together was a glorious one.

The spirit of the Ashram may be gathered from the mottoes on the wall of our meeting room: "Leave behind all race and class distinction ye that enter here"—we felt the Kingdom of God is race- and class-blind, so our society must also be. Another motto:

> "Here we enter a fellowship;
> Sometimes we will agree to differ;
> Always we will resolve to love,
> And unite to serve."

We deliberately determined that we would not make the fellowship out of people of one type of mentality, so we provided for difference—the theologically, politically, and the economically conservative and the radical would be brought together to cross-fertilize each other mentally and spiritually. If our fellowship could only be maintained as long as we all signed on the dotted line in every detail of faith and outlook, the fellowship would be an immature hothouse affair unable to stand up under the stress of life. This difference would include the non-Christian who would be a real part of our fellowship, entering into our meetings and devotions as far as he felt he could, but without any compulsions. Not that we are syncretic. We are not. Christ is the center without apology and without compromise, but the Christ we are trying to live and present is not the Christ of dogmatism, or communalism, or racialism. He is the Son of man, at home amid the sons of men.

Another motto: "East and West are alternate beats of the same heart." We know that East needs West and West needs East, and perhaps out of the twain shall come a new man in Christ. Another: "There is no philosophy or religion possible where fear of consequences is a greater incentive than love of truth." We determined that no inhibiting fear of consequences should cramp our thinking and our quest. We should follow truth as blind men long for light.

A motto that had real consequences is this one:

> "Fellowship is based on confidence;
> Secret criticism breaks that confidence;
> We will, therefore, renounce all secret criticism."

This was very penetrating, for we interpreted it as meaning that we would not hold any mental criticism of each other without bringing it to the one concerned. We would not only not secretly express criticism, we would not hold any at all without bringing it up. We would be on a basis of complete frankness. If there were no outward criticism, then we would know there was no inward, hence, all questionings and strain would be taken out of the atmosphere, and the fellowship would be free, relaxed, and real. There would be no hard knots of unresolved relationships around which we would vainly try to have fellowship. And the fellowship would be deep because we would be fellowshiping at the depths and not merely in petty surface politenesses. The willingness to take criticism in the right spirit is perhaps the deepest sign of grace one can have, for it touches the quick, the self, and if we are unsurrendered there, we will resent it and begin to defend ourselves. An attitude of defense is an attitude of fear, and where there is fear there is no fellowship. This willingness to take criticism must extend across the usual barriers of race and class and color. One must be open to the suggestions of even the weakest. A convert of a few months said this to me one day: "Brother Stanley, I've noticed that when we give you a question or problem which you can't really answer, you take us off to something very interesting and make us forget the point. Is this honest?" I have profited by that straightforward word, and now when I am tempted to duck into some open door out of a problem, I am learning to say, "I don't know." Another incident helped me. A man turned on me in public print with an unjust criticism to which I wrote a devastating reply in a few lines. But before I sent off the reply, I forwarded it to the Ashram group to get their reaction. They prayerfully considered it and wrote three words on the margin and sent it back: "Not sufficiently redemptive." I was winning my argument, but I was losing my man, and the business of the Christian is not to win arguments but to win people. They were right—our actions must all be redemptive. Alongside of many things we do and say we can write the words, "Not sufficiently redemptive." So I tore up my reply and made none at all. I would leave my reputation with God. A few weeks later I received a letter from this man saying, "Today is New Year's Day, and I'm trying to straighten up things; forgive me for the things I wrote in the paper about you." I am quite sure my reply would never have produced that result. The group's frank and objective criticism of my reply helped me to see the matter in the Christian perspective. How poor we are when we have no such conspiracy of love! Of course the danger is that we may become mote-pickers, and yet the knowledge that we must say these things to each other, and the further knowledge that we must be prepared to receive criticism, act as restraints. Another motto tries to correct this tendency to mote-picking:

"When about to criticize another ask four questions:
1. Is it true?
2. Is it necessary?
3. Is it kind?
4. Is it redemptive?"

When we come into the Ashram as members, we lay aside all titles. There are no more bishops, doctors, professors, there are just persons. We call each other by our first name, "Brother Stanley, Brother Rama, Sister Mary, Sister Lila." It has a real psychological effect on one to be called by one's first name. It is not easy to be high and mighty when someone is calling you "Brother Stanley." It has a very real leveling effect. The word "Brother" and "Sister" added to it has "an antiseptic effect on our relationships," as a Hindu member of our group put it. Besides, if we are a Family of God, what true or nobler words could describe our relationships?

And that is just what we try to be—a Family of God, a demonstration in miniature of the meaning of the Kingdom of God. People must not only hear about the Kingdom of God, but must see it in actual operation, on a small scale perhaps, and in imperfect form, but a real demonstration nevertheless. Little islands of cooperation amid the raging seas of competition are what is needed. "You are a Family of God," said a Hindu sadhu one day as he was about to leave after a day with us. I was surprised, for he did not understand a word of our language, and when I expressed my surprise he replied, "Yes, but I can see by your joy and freedom that you are a Family of God."

As a Family of God, we have chosen certain disciplines for the Home. We have chosen them—they are not imposed. The rising bell goes at five-thirty, and we go out to the prayer knoll for our morning devotions, which are opened by a hymn and closed by a hymn, but in between we are in corporate silence. We are trying to rediscover the power of silence which our Quaker friends know so well. To become silent is a real test of resources. Many run through their resources in a very few moments of silence. To be able "to draw water out of your own well" is a very real test. Many find their buckets scraping on the bottom in a short time. We try to make life so full that this will not happen. At the close of this hour of meditation, we march back singing a processional hymn, written for the occasion, telling how we come out of the prayer hour to greet the day with a song and with God. When we arrive at the Ashram, the leader turns and raises his hand and says, "The Lord is risen," and the group, with raised right hands, answer, "He is risen indeed." It is in the radiancy and power of the risen Christ that we go into the day.

We then have our early morning meal, which is eaten in Indian style, seated cross-legged on the floor—even stiff European legs can get used to it after awhile! Flowing Indian clothes make it easier. To wear Indian clothes is not compulsory, but customary. That too has a psychological effect. I cannot explain, but you simply do feel different toward India when wearing Indian clothes. I suppose this can be explained by the fact that when doing so, you step over to the other side of things. For there are two sides in India—the dominating and the dominated. To put on Indian clothes makes you take your stand with the dominated. It is a real renunciation. And many of the West resent a member of their group doing it. "Don't the Europeans dislike your wearing Indian clothes?" asked a questioner at Question Time. "Yes," I said, "I suppose so. That's one reason why I do it." Not that one wants to be cantankerous with his racial group, but he wants to master this racial arrogance within himself.

We began wearing Indian clothes at Sat Tal during the tense days of political agitation, and since we wore homespun khaddar cloth, it made us politically suspect as well. We knew that spies were in our fellowship. When I went to see the Viceroy, I found his secretary with my complete record. I saw then that I would have to see the head of the C. I. D. (the secret police) and go over things with him. I did. I told him that I was sympathetic toward India's national aspirations, that I had stayed with Mahatma Gandhi, that I had attended the National Congress, that I received questions at the Question Hour in my public meetings which I could not dodge and have any moral authority—questions which had political bearing; but I gave him my word of honor that I was not taking any part in politics as such, but that I was an evangelist going to men as men, including the nationalists, with my message of Christ and His Kingdom. He was very sympathetic toward my position. It cleared the atmosphere. The next day when some C. I. D. men were taking down notes of my address on the Sermon on the Mount to see whether it was seditious (!) I told them at the close that they need not bother, that I had seen their boss and he knew the whole truth. Another C. I. D. man, who came to my address to spy, stayed to pray, and was converted!

But back to the Ashram program. On the whole, we wear Indian clothes at the Ashram, but some members do not. I, personally, do not wear them all the time

when I am away from the Ashram, but feel free to wear
them whenever I am impelled. Almost always when I
wear them in public meetings, a change comes over the
audience—the atmosphere is friendlier, often enthusiastic.
This is not always true of Westernized Indians, especially
Westernized Indian Christians, who perhaps feel the
wearing of Indian clothes is a silent judgment on their
lack of nationalism and as such they may resent it.

At the close of the morning meal, we have a work
period to which we go after singing our work song:

> "O Thou who long didst labor,
>   With hammer, saw, and plane,
> Help us this day to serve Thee,
>   With hands and heart and brain,
> In toil we fain would find Thee
>   O Workman, strong and fair,
> And thus become the comrades
>   Of workers everywhere."

To work with one's hands in India is not considered respectable; no gentleman does it. That is why we do it.
And when we do it, we are in line with that new stream
of thought in India in which work is not only respectable
but highly patriotic. It is a fine discipline to have bishops,
government officials, Brahmins, and the rest of us working
side by side. And the sisters too, one of whom wrote
some poetry on the work period, every line of which ended,
"O my sisters, see my blisters."

At the close of the work period we have two hours of
corporate thinking. We study a subject each summer,
the one this summer being, "Christian Realism in Rela-
tion to the Kingdom of God, the Church, and India."
There are two ways to approach questions—one the competitive way of thinking in which you push your idea
forward, argue it, put it to a vote and the majority rules.
But this always leaves a disgruntled minority which feels

its truth has been lost sight of. The other way is the method of cooperative thinking, in which we start from the presupposition that none of us hold the truth. The truth is Christ, the incarnate Truth. What we hold is truths about the Truth. We must, therefore, pool our truths so that our pooled truths might more closely approximate the Truth. In this way we come away with a larger truth than the one we brought to it. This has happened because we start with all barriers down. In competitive thinking we start with barriers up and usually end our discussions behind higher barriers. Out of this group thinking we usually produce a book.

An interesting fact has emerged from these ten years at Sat Tal. Although the tension between East and West is very strong in India and men almost invariably think along racial lines, yet in our group never once has the discussion divided up with the Indians on one side and the Westerners on the other. Where there has been a division of thought, it has always been between conservative and radical. This is a division that runs through all races on all subjects, for the human mind breaks up into these two great types. This is important for places like South Africa and the United States, where men fear the colored races will stand on one side and the white on the other on all public questions. They will if there are disabilities in any group which will drive them together through resentment. But where there is equality of treatment between racial groups, and thought is free, the conservatives of the colored races will line up with the conservatives of the white race, and the radicals with the radicals.

This division of the human mind into radical and conservative is beneficial, for if we were all conservatives, we should dry up; and if we were all radicals, we should blow up! Between the pull-back of the conservative and the pull-ahead of the radical we make progress in a middle direction. The Kingdom of God has use for both, for it says, "The disciple to the kingdom of God is like a householder who brings forth from his treasure things new and old." Note the "new and old"—both. But the "new" was first, for the Kingdom is primarily radical since it stands for the great Change. But it gathers up and conserves the old on the way to the New.

One day a week we have a day of complete silence. This we learned from Mahatma Gandhi, a custom which has probably saved his life. It certainly has done something for us. After talking to each other for six days, there is an immense sense of relief to have one day to oneself when no one raises a question or presents an issue. For that day our souls are our own. Most of us go to the forest that day with a book and prayer in order to consolidate our spiritual gains.

Another day of the week we give the few servants we have a holiday, and we volunteer to take their places. To get volunteers for the cook's job is not difficult, for even in caste-ridden India the cook's job is fairly respectable. Brahmins cook. But the sweeper's job includes the cleaning of the latrines—for we do not have the flush system—and only the lowest of the low-caste men will do this work. But we have felt that we have no right to allow this man to do this degrading work unless we are willing to share it with him, so we ask for volunteers from among the men—not an easy thing to do, either for the brown Brahmins of India or the white Brahmins of the West. But it is a spiritual discipline to do it. One high English official among us said: "Now when I want to give my servant a holiday, I give him eight annas [sixteen cents] to get a substitute. Why wouldn't that suffice?" It really does not suffice, for while it would satisfy the legalities, it would not satisfy the Christian conscience. Our work degrades the sweeper, therefore we must share that degradation. We have been criticized at this point a good deal, for, it is objected, we are throwing away our prestige. Perhaps we are. And yet we must cease to worship at the shrine of the great god Prestige if we are Kingdom-of-God men. For in the Kingdom we do not become great through conserving of prestiges but by becoming the servants of all. But does it throw away prestige? Actually I have not found it so. The first day we sent away the sweeper for his holiday and we took his work, at eventide I looked through my window and there was the sweeper standing with folded hands in the manner of worship, his face wreathed in smiles. He too was a man—our taking his place had made him such. The crust of custom of centuries had been broken and a man was emerging. That smiling face was worth it all. We have had servants come and touch our feet, in obeisance, and then I realized that having lost prestige we had found it again, this time the real thing. But some of our group still hesitate to take the step across the gulf. One Brahmin convert replied when I asked him when he were going to volunteer, "Brother Stanley, I'm converted, but I'm not converted that far." Our conversions are very limited! We must extend the area of our conversions until they include the whole of life. I suppose I feel strongly about this doing the sweeper's work from an incident, when, as a young missionary, I sat with the headman of a village and talked to him about Christ and the sweeper went past us carrying human excreta in his bare hands from the headman's house. I inwardly burned with shame, for the sweeper had been baptized by me a few days before and human custom had compelled him to do this! Until the growth of modern conveniences takes this degrading work from his hands, I must share with my brother his degradations.

But the deepest identification with the underprivileged which I have come across, and one that makes our momentary identifications seem trivial, was one which one of our present Ashram staff members carried through. He is highly educated, a graduate of Cambridge, a lawyer and a Brahmin of South India—they are the Brahmins of the Brahmins, many of whom are not only untouchable, but unseeable when they eat. His grandfather was so Brahmanically orthodox that when a grandchild's clothes caught fire he refused to touch her because he had just ceremonially purified himself while the child had not, so she burned to death before other help could come. An uncle fell into a well, and when an outcaste rushed to rescue him, he refused the help lest he be polluted by the touch of the outcaste, and was drowned—a martyr to caste. This was the kind of Brahmanism from which he came. Before he became a Christian he was so indignant with this system of caste that he went to the outcaste quarter, had the eligible marriage women lined up and, as he puts it, "picking out the blackest and most uncouth one among them," he asked her to marry him. She did, and when she died he married her sister who is now an honored member of our Ashram. He was sentenced six times and spent six years in jail as a follower of Mahatma Gandhi during the national struggle. The Mahatma gave him a copy of the Gita, Tolstoy, and the New Testament to read while in jail. The jailor stamped on the New Testament, "Not dangerous"! He came out of jail a convinced Christian—converted by the gift of the Mahatma, who, although he does not believe in conversion, was the instrument of a conversion. A real one too.

Perhaps the fellowship across caste and class lines is not more wonderful than that across the chasm of political division. I saw a young nationalist clad in nationalist homespun go off for a conversation with a British Resident, a man who was the Imperial Government representative over twenty Indian States. When they returned, I asked the young nationalist how he had got on. His face lighted up as he said: "He is a wonderful man. I didn't know the Government had men in it like that." Then I asked the official, and his reply was almost identical: "I was delighted with him. I didn't know the nationalist movement had men like that in it." They had discovered each other. That same British official learned at the Ashram that he could be used of God to help an Indian into victory. He thought God could only use him among his own people. But having the glorious experience he was like a tiger that had tasted human blood for the first time—he wanted more! Another young nationalist told how this official had won him: "I hid behind one bush after another, but he beat me out of one hiding place to another, and finally he got me." His life since then shows that he had "got" him. An interesting sidelight was in the fact that this young man had also been in jail as a follower of Gandhi—pursued by the British Government from "bush to bush" and landed in jail. There is no question as to which of the British methods was the more effective.

Seldom does anyone go away from the Ashram unchanged. For with all our trying to adjust ourselves to India there is a central and driving desire to get people who come to us adjusted to Christ. Everything converges on that. The various approaches head up there. The Oxford Group movement adherents and all the rest of us drive toward that goal. By the way, I think we have shown the possibility of having the Oxford Group work as an integral part of the Ashram, but without the tragic divisions set up in some places. We throw everything open for the Groupers to get hold of anyone they can. And they have genuinely helped many. But we have the understanding that neither they, nor any other group, are the Kingdom; that is beyond us all. We are only more or less approximations of that Kingdom and instruments of its coming. Moreover, the Oxford Group is not the issue—Christ is. Behind Christ the Group is a wonderful instrument, in front of Christ it is a point of false division and contention. I refuse to allow the question of my belonging or not belonging to any Group to become an issue. Whether I belong to Christ or not is an issue—a real one and the only one. On that basis I am free to fellowship with Oxford Groupers in the same way I would fellowship with any other Christians? In most things I find a very deep affinity with them. I state my one point of reservation very frankly, and then we get on with the work as fellow Christians. For they probably have reservations about the Ashram and me. Someone wrote from England to a friend in India: "Are you a follower of Weatherhead and Stanley Jones, or are you a Christian?" I was happy with my company! An evangelist in India felt impelled, so he said, to fight four things: "The Oxford Group movement, the Indian National Congress, Kagawa, and Stanley Jones." Again I was glad of my company. And as I sat down with this evangelist I found I had many things in common with him too. And I refused to shut him out of my fellowship, whatever he did with me.

At the meeting by the lakeside as the evening shadows fall over the emerald beauty of the waters, we are again and again brought into saving contact with Christ. The several hundred who sit there look above the head of the speaker to the cross planted in the cleared place on the opposite mountainside. It was a courageous thing to plant that cross there amid that jungle. For the deer come to get a drink at eventide with stealthy tread, alert at every step, lest a lurking tiger or a leopard pounce upon its graceful form. This year a woman cutting grass upon a near-by hill was killed by a tiger and eaten almost entirely, and when the friends and relatives came to gather up the remnants of her body to carry to the burning ghat, the tiger, waiting near by for his second meal, objected to the remnants being taken away—they were his by right of conquest, so he uttered a growl of protest, and the villagers dropped the precious bits and fled in terror. To put a cross in the midst of that! And yet we felt that this was the very place to put it. For today we are compelled to plant the cross in the midst of civilization turning jungle, where tiger nations swallow smaller ones and growl over remnants which they say is theirs by right of conquest. On that opposite hillside two forces struggle for the mastery—lower nature and the cross— the struggle for life and the struggle for the life of others. As we sit there in full view of the tragedy and pain in nature we bet our lives on the cross. After all, the tiger and the leopard are slowly but surely being exterminated —their end is in sight. They took the sword as their way of life and they are perishing by the sword. So it will be with nations who take the same way—as they take the sword they will perish with the sword. So with confidence we plant the cross high above that jungle, and even though one night a wild animal pushed it over crooked we set it straight again, knowing that that cross held the future. And it must hold us—*now*.

On Sunday morning we have communion given one Sunday by an Anglican and the next by a Free Churchman. And *mirable dictu* the High Churchman not only gives it to us, but takes it from us. In that communion we have everyone from the High Churchman to the Quaker and all types between. And sometimes we have unbaptized Hindus partaking of it with us. I knew that was not very orthodox, but I felt it was very Christian, for these Hindus were committed to Christ as their Lord and

Saviour and confessed Him before us, but had not yet come into the Christian Church. One day one minister refused to give communion to one of these "informal Christians," and the next Sunday as I gave communion to them both, it happened they were kneeling side by side. After all, they were in the same deep need of Christ's atoning blood.

Most of our baptisms are done through the Churches, but sometimes we baptize in the Ashram itself. In several such baptisms we anticipated Church unity by having clergymen of the Lutheran, the Church of England, and the Methodist denominations baptize the candidates with a corporate baptism, each laying hands on him and baptizing him simultaneously. From the beginning they belonged to us all! And then we sent each one back to a particular denomination to be nurtured.

At the close of the communion we have "A Meeting of the Open Heart," in which we really let each other into the inner secrets, we share to the depths. Here we really begin to know each other. How often we are alongside of each other and yet know so little of each other! "I have been alongside of my colleagues here for years and never knew they were going through these struggles and battles until this morning," said a professor at the close of a Round Table Conference. That often happens between Christian workers, and in this morning meeting we try to get to the center of our problems. Here many find release and power.

"This whole Sat Tal is a vast graveyard," said a young man as he was about to leave. "It is full of the graves of our dead selves. I am leaving a grave behind me and going back a new man." Another put it this way: "I came here a flickering torch and I am going away a flaming torch." To set each one on fire so they will go back to their places in India and put into operation the new spirit found here—this is a real part of our task. Said an English lady: "As I came through the mountain pass into Sat Tal, I felt a spirit, a sense of awe, of God; it is holy ground." It is. And we can never be too grateful for what it has meant to us and others.

But we soon found our rejoicing giving way to questionings. This fellowship in Sat Tal is the most beautiful I have ever seen, and yet our hearts sank at the thought that we were not meeting the real issue—the economic. That was the serpent we found in our paradise. There is little use trying to achieve fellowship over or around unjust economic relationships. It will block your fellowship at every turn. There must be a basic justice in relationships, or else religion becomes mere charity, and charity without justice is an insult. True, we charged for board to visitors one rupee and eight annas a day (fifty cents) for those whose salaries are over one hundred rupees per month and half that, twelve annas (twenty-five cents), a day for those whose salaries are below, with the same food and lodging. And some students we take for eight annas (sixteen cents) a day. We thus try to make the financially strong bear the infirmities of the weak. But we all had our economic roots in the plains, and our fellowship in the mountains did not touch that vital fact.

This word "fellowship" is a terribly demanding and disturbing word. We think we have satisfied it, and then it begins to ask questions about compartments not yet possessed by it. It is like the word "democracy." We think we have safely confined it to the political, and then it begins to ask questions as to why it should not be extended to the social and economic as well. And when the question is asked in the flaming tongues of a Russian revolution, we are compelled to take notice.

So we began to ask the question of whether this fellowship was possible in the heart of a great city, and could it include the economic? If not, your Kingdom-of-God order works only in the airy spiritual and not in terms of the hard material. If that be so, it is useless as a working way of life, for the nerve center of our world problem is the economic. If that place cannot be Christianized, then we abdicate at the center and try to rule at the margin with a half-Christ ruling over a half-Kingdom.

But I was an evangelist, and while I could fit in Sat Tal with my summer months when traveling was well-nigh impossible in the burning plains, how could I fit into my evangelism a full-time Ashram at Lucknow? How could I undertake the financial burden involved? Still the relentlessness of the demand would brook no denial. I would have to make the group of workers responsible for the running of it, and I would come and go as my evangelistic work allowed. The demonstration of the Kingdom-of-God order must be attempted, however imperfect it might be. There must be no attempt to make a halfway house a home. We had to go on.

It was while studying the Nazareth Manifesto of Jesus at Sat Tal that the Lucknow Ashram was born. The Ashram would be an attempt to make that Manifesto real. The economic basis had to be faced at once. Since we were attempting a Kingdom-of-God society, we would try to find the economic basis of the Kingdom of God. This we found in the Acts of the Apostles to be: "Distribution was made according to each one's necessities." Distribution according to need seemed an ultimate basis. This came out of an experience of God at Pentecost, the natural, normal extension of spirituality into the economic. But how to arrive at each one's needs? Who is to determine the basis of need? Three factors are involved: God, the individual, and the group.

Each one who was to be a permanent member of the staff was asked to go aside, preferably on the day of silence, and, in the presence of God and of his own conscience, make out his budget of minimum need. Food and lodging were to be the same for all, but beyond those two things needs differed. The basis of judging need would be: We have a right to use as much of the material as will make us more fit for the purposes of the Kingdom of God. A certain amount of material things do make us more fit, beyond that amount; they clog us, they become impedimenta. Material things for use, and use in the Kingdom of God—that is the criterion. The latter is important, for use in the Kingdom of God might differ radically from use in a society with other standards and aims.

Moreover, there must be some relationship to the surrounding life, for one has to function in those surroundings. There cannot be too great a divergence from the surrounding life when that life is economically low, or else one can be of little use to the people concerned.

We have discovered that there are two ways to be rich —one is in the abundance of your possessions and the other is in the fewness of your wants. We strive to be rich in the latter way. To be able to do without a thing grandly is riches.

When the budget of need is made out, it is presented to the group which goes over it prayerfully, item by item. It is easier now, for we have learned by testing it out what a normal expenditure should be for clothes, etc. When it is approved by the group it is in operation, but can be periodically revised up or down. Those of us who are not at the Ashram all the time report our expenditures to the group.

A strange thing happens in a cooperative society—the mentality changes. In a competitive order each man tries to put up his allowance as far as possible and the other man tries to push it down as far as possible—a compromise is effected and a working agreement arrived at. But in this cooperative order we find that each man in loyalty to the group desires to keep his allowance as low as possible. Wherever we have had suggestions to make for change in a budget, it has almost always been on the basis that it was too low. A few exceptions, but that has been the usual experience. The average allowance for a single person, Westerner or Indian, beyond food and lodging, is eight dollars to twelve dollars per month. A married couple with, say, two children will average about twenty dollars to thirty dollars. The food cost averages about twenty cents a day per person. Food values have been worked out scientifically, so the group keeps robust and healthy on this. The food is partly Western and partly Indian.

To arrive at a common diet would seem not easy when our group is composed at present of people of the following nationalities: Turkestani, Arab, Danish, Afghan, American (white and Negro), Punjabi, Marathi, Malayali, Javanese, Finnish, Hindustani, Tamil, Garhwali, and others. Our English, Dutch, and Australian members are absent for the moment. The classes represented stretch all the way from the Afghan prince to the depressed class group. While one would think that the difference in accustomed diet would be so great that it would be impossible to arrive at a common diet, yet, in fact, we have not found it so. We have now a diet which seems satisfying to all. Not only is the brain of humanity one, the stomach of humanity is also one.

In our fellowship the reader will have noted that we have married people. This differs from the outstanding Christian Ashrams at Poona and Tirrupatur, where only single persons are accepted on the staff. This taking of only single persons makes the task easier in some ways, and fits in with the great work these Ashrams are doing, and yet we felt that our experiment would not be complete unless it included all the elements that make up human society. We would have to fit the family into our fellowship. But to do so we would have to give sufficient freedom to the family consciousness, consistent with group life. To do this, we allow the family to take as many meals separately during the day as they feel will conserve the family life. The rest of the meals are taken with the group. We find that children brought up under this corporate living develop a strong social sense and an at-homeness with all races; at the same time the family ties do not appear to be diminished in the slightest.

As for social security, we have the provision that dependents of deceased members become a first charge on the budget—they are as secure as the group itself is secure. The finances are met by the group raising as much as possible, and I meet the deficits partly from income from my books and partly from the help of friends. We have the rule that there shall be no debts. If we have not the money, we do not spend it. The property is held for us by the Executive Board of The Methodist Church, but the Ashram is an interdenominational Ashram—an excellent example of how one denomination can allow interdenominational experimentation within itself. Baptisms of converts is usually administered in the various Churches and not in the Ashram. We have no desire to set up another denomination.

When each person's needs are met, then he is to give in service to the group and to surrounding society according to his ability. "If a man will not work, neither shall he eat," is Pauline and proper. We work out into the various needs of the life of the city. We have the following departments: 1. Home management. 2. Medical work with a local dispensary and a traveling medical bus which goes to the villages in the afternoons and carries medical help to the neediest place of the world—the Indian village.

3. Newspaper Evangelism, in which Christian evangelistic articles are put in daily papers and correspondence with inquirers carried on. 4. Postal Evangelism, in which we send Christian literature to about thirty-five hundred leaders of the depressed classes throughout India. 5. Women's work. 6. Public contacts, through which we get in touch with the national leaders, especially as Lucknow is the center of the United Provinces Government which is now Nationalist. 7. Literature, one member being set aside for the production of Christian literature with an Indian flavor. 8. Student work, there is no Y. M. C. A. or Y. W. C. A. in this university and college center. 9. Training of a new type of Christian servant for India—the Kristagrahis, "men of Christ-force." 10. Literacy campaign—we provide literature for the semiliterates to keep them literate. 11. Dealing with inquirers who come to study Christianity. 12. A language school in which new missionaries start their career with right attitudes toward India and respect for Indian culture and brains. 13. Village center and Mohulla center to be developed as next steps.

Above all, we try to make the Ashram atmosphere such that Christians and non-Christians coming in contact with it will find what they need.

We started with no fixed constitution. We began with the doors open to be led as the Spirit would give us corporate guidance. After three years of experimentation we saw our general directions and spirit and wrote down a constitution. While we are now fixed, we are flexible and ready for new urges of the Spirit and new calls of service.

All our decisions are made by the group. We believe that a group can become "an organism of the Holy Spirit." We made a motto: "Let this Group be an Organism of the Holy Spirit," and gave it to an artist friend to paint. He could not believe we meant the above and put it: "Let this Group be an Organization of the Holy Spirit." So many of our institutions and movements are only organizations—things brought together, and not organisms, things possessed of a spirit and function.

To get collective guidance in our decisions we have worked out the following technique: 1. When a matter is presented, we go into silence, letting down all the barriers so that the Spirit can speak to us on the matter in hand. 2. Then we go round the circle and ask each one's view. This is done so that no strong person might unduly influence the group by speaking first. We need the total group thought. 3. If, in going round, we find there is practical unanimity, we go into silence again before taking the vote to be sure we ought to vote now. If we are sure, then, 4. The vote is taken. But that vote is not taken unless there is practical unanimity about the matter and about the matter being settled now.

If there is not practical unanimity, then we put off the voting until the next day to see if we can get further light. If we cannot come to a common mind, and the matter must be settled, then we finally resort to a majority vote as a last resort.

I have attended committee meetings all my life in which the competitive attitude underlies the discussions. Men come with barriers up and arguments ready. God forgive me the hours I have wasted in this kind of thing! On the other hand, when we come with the cooperative mentality, with barriers down, with the eager desire to come to a common mind, we can get through twice as much business in a given time. And we can arise at the close feeling that we have undergone a spiritual experience of God.

Please do not misunderstand me. It has not all been sweetness and light. There have been failures in spirit and technique and outcome. Often it has been a painfully inadequate attempt to express the overwhelming vision.

We have often had to ask pardon of one another for wrong attitudes and words. We have been accused of being "self-righteous." We have many sins, but this one is our least difficulty, for I know no group more self-critical, relentlessly so. One member fasted for two days, for he felt there had been a let-down in spirit in the group. Our greatest difficulty is to make our mysticism practical, to make it have insight into human need and then roll up its sleeves and tackle that need with a tenacity that knows no turning back. Most all of us have been idealists and talkers all our lives and to turn talking idealists into working realists is no easy task. We often get tangled in a web of lovely words and never get beyond them. And the Indian does not help our weakness at this point. India has been described as "a nation of good listeners." Philosophy thrived in India because philosophy dealt with ideas. You can raise an Indian audience off its seat in appreciation and applause, and then when you ask them whether they will do something about it, they will reply, "Oh, no, but it's all very lovely and we will hear you again." Idealists, who link up with philosophers to undertake to put into operation the Kingdom of God on earth are bound to have trouble and disillusionments. We have had both.

But we are undeterred by both, for we can discipline ourselves to realism, and no discouragement can turn us back from following what we have seen and heard. For amid it all has come the settled conviction that we have discovered something that has the feel of the ultimate upon it. Strip off the name "Ashram" and its Indian framework and you have a basis for living which can be universalized. A group living together in cooperative fellowship under a common purpose, with physical needs met and each giving to the collective good according to his ability, is an ultimate way to live. And when a group does so live together, it becomes a cell of the Kingdom of God.

Alexis Carrel in his great book, *Man, the Unknown,* working from the scientific standpoint toward a way of life comes out to the place where he advocates the formation of small groups of highly trained men who shall live in simplicity and single-minded devotion to the collective good and who shall think through the problems of human living and give guidance to humanity in its confusion and blundering. Science had led him to the same place to which we had been led in India.

The world-order is in the midst of a rapid decay. It may be that after the collapse little groups of various kinds dotted here and there across the world may contain the germs of a new order, may become the seed plots from which will spring up a new civilization. If so, we must have our little plot ready, for we want that new order to be the Kingdom-of-God order. Patiently we must pull out the weeds, for they are many, and they choke the new life, and we must water the seeds sometimes with our tears and sometimes even with our hearts' blood, ever keeping the sense of destiny upon us. For did not Jesus say, "The good seed is the sons of the kingdom?"

He defined the seed as the sons of the Kingdom. One was called in the Hebrew idiom the son of something when the quality of that something was uppermost in him. Judas was called "the son of perdition," Barnabas, "the son of consolation," John and James "sons of thunder," and Jesus "the Son of God." Men saw hell in Judas, consolation in Barnabas, thunder in James and John, and God in Jesus. So men shall see in other men "sons of the kingdom" for the Kingdom is the center of their loyalty, the master light of all their seeing and the fact of their redemption. These sons of the Kingdom hold the Kingdom as the hope of the world and demonstrate it in their individual and corporate lives, and they, though they be buried in obscure plots, are to become the seed of a new age to come. We have no illusions about being one of those plots, but we also have no hesitation in saying that it is exactly what we would like to be, and perhaps by His grace may be.

CHAPTER IX

I CAME NEAR MISSING MY WAY

I BEGAN this book by telling how I first got my feet upon the Indian Road, and now I must end by telling why I keep them there. But first I must tell you how I came near ceasing to be an evangelist along that Road.

I think the word "evangelist," the bearer of good tidings, the most beautiful word in our language descriptive of vocation. I have been tempted to desert the name, for it has fallen on evil days and has a bad odor, but I have never been able to let it go, for it would not let me go. I remember when applying for a visa to go into Russia, I was asked by the Soviet representative about my vocation. When I told him his face became clouded and puzzled. Seeing this, I said brightly, "Well, put me down as 'Lecturer.'" "Yes, that's better. That will do," he replied. The word "lecturer" was more respectable, but when I looked at it I could not thrill over it, nor feel the depth of call as I do when I look at the word "evangelist." When I have been tempted to assume the lecturer attitude, I have always miserably failed. I remember coming back to India from a study of Europe, and that the very first night after my arrival I gave a lecture on European conditions. I got all tangled up with myself and others; it was a miserable performance. The bitter lesson was learned, so the next night I slipped back into my native element and was at home and free. For a night I had been a prodigal. Now I was back in my Father's house. The Pharisees tempted Jesus "to speak of many things"—many things that would take Him off the central thing. Beware when you are tempted to speak of many things!

But these little upsets were nothing to a crisis which

came to me on a trip to America to attend the General
Conference of the Methodist Episcopal Church. My work
is interdenominational, for the Methodist mission has very
graciously kept me as their missionary and yet has let
me free to work with all missions for twenty-four years.
But I have rejoiced in the Methodist fellowship. It is a
wonderful fellowship. In China some Christians were
captured by bandits and held for a ransom. The missionary went to the bandit chief to remonstrate with him, saying, "Why don't you let these people go? they're Christians." "Christians?" said the bandit, in surprise. "What
kind of Christians?" When told they were Methodists,
the bandit replied, warmly, "Of course, I'll let them go.
I'm a Methodist too." It's a great fellowship!

But, seriously, I was glad to turn aside from my interdenominational work and go to the General Conference,
little knowing the crisis which would confront me there.
When the voting began for the election of bishops I with-
drew my name, as I had withdrawn it before at a previous
General Conference. I honored, loved, and respected
bishops and believed in them, but it was not my calling.
I was an evangelist and must stick to my last. But the
withdrawal did not settle matters. When a deadlock
between the two contestants for the bishopric came after
twenty ballots, some one proposed the astounding proposal that the secretary cast the ballot for me. My first
impulse was to rise and say the matter was settled, that
I would withdraw my name again. But as I was about
to do so, to my astonishment, the Inner Voice said im-
periously, "Don't touch it." I have always depended on
that Voice in every crisis, and it has always been right.
It has never let me down. And now it was so clear that
I dared not go against it. I sat still and heard the presiding
bishop rule out of order the motion for the secretary to
cast the ballot—the balloting must proceed. At the next

ballot I was elected. In the wave of emotion that swept across the vast assembly I was swept away from my moorings. I felt for the time that perhaps God was using this emotional upheaval to break down my hesitations and that the bishopric really was my work. After the session I cabled my wife in India: "Unmistakably led accept bishopric." When she received the cable, it was a blow to her and plunged her into deep depression of spirit. Still, there was the word "unmistakably" to hold on to, and she held on to that amid the darkness and perplexity.

But the word "unmistakably" soon became very shaky to me as I tossed all night upon my bed. By morning it was gone. A mistake had been made and I knew it. I was headed in the wrong direction. I chanced to overhear one delegate say to another at breakfast in a restaurant, "Wasn't there a mistake made last night?" "Yes, there was," I inwardly replied with the heaviest heart a man can bear in his bosom.

My perplexity was not only over a mistake being made in my life's work. One can survive even a mistake of that kind and live. My perplexity was deeper: I had listened to the Inner Voice, which was clear and imperious, and by listening to it I had landed in this utter darkness. If I could not depend on the Inner Voice in a crisis like that, what could I depend on? It struck a blow at the very foundations of my spiritual life. I was like a man whose universe had suddenly turned all wrong. I wrote out my resignation, but could find no place to present it during the day, nor did I find any impulse to do so. I was hedged in—I could not go on, nor did I see how I could go back. To go back seemed like letting the Conference down. After all, they had given me the greatest honor in their power to give—an honor for which I felt no right or fitness. It had all turned to ashes in my hands.

When people came up and called me "Bishop," and

when telegrams of congratulation poured in, it all stabbed me like a knife. My face must have shown my utter misery, for I could feel the great drops of sweat upon my brow. I revealed my heart to only one man, a trusted and loved bishop, and his reply was: "You've got to go on, no matter how you feel. The Church will think you fickle and will no longer follow your lead if you don't go on. You must sacrifice your own way at the call of the Church." Arm in arm with my own beloved Bishop Robinson I was taken into the Board of Bishops to be welcomed into that fraternity. I should have been thrilled to be in the company of such men. Instead I felt like rising and saying: "Brothers, I do not belong here. I am an evangelist and not a bishop. Let me go back to my task in India." But the words could not be spoken. The fact is I was writing my resignation to the Board of Bishops when I was interrupted by the bishop telling me I had to go in now to be welcomed. I can see now that to try to resign before them would have been wrong procedure— they had not elected me and could not receive my resignation. But the attempt to write that resignation in the antechamber was symbolic of the chaotic thinking which came out of my chaotic soul.

The next day was the Consecration, and the ceremony, very solemn and impressive, had to be practiced. This was the hardest thing of all. I felt like a condemned man going to his execution as I walked up the aisle in stately procession. It was so utterly unreal to me.

The night meeting of Saturday came and it was the very last opportunity of my getting out before consecration, which was to be on Sunday. And if I got out at all, it would have to be in the first hour of the session, for I had to leave at nine o'clock to get the last train to Saint Joseph —I was to have the sunrise service in the public park on Pentecost morning. As I got to the platform my Inner

Voice, silent all day, came back: "Now is the time to get out," it said. For the first time in nearly twenty-four hours confidence came back. I went straight to the chairman, Bishop Johnson, and said I had a matter of high privilege. Business was pressing and he refused to allow me the floor unless I told him what it was. I saw I would have to let him know and pushed my resignation in front of him. He had to let me go on. I read my resignation, thanked them for the high honor, but felt I must go back an evangelist in India. I walked straight off the platform, out of the building at the back and down the street to my train. I did not wait to see if my resignation would be accepted. I was hastening to get back to the Indian Road—as an evangelist. What mattered if I was an outcaste from my beloved Church, as the bishop had predicted I would be. I was ready for that or for anything else. I walked on air as I strode toward the station. When I arrived at Saint Joseph, the pastor greeted me as "Bishop." I stopped him: "That was terminated an hour ago," I said. "Thank God," he replied, "for any number of people have called me up today and suggested that it had been a mistake to elect you a bishop." "Yes, it had been a mistake," I assented, almost too full of joy to speak.

But as I look back, I see that there was not a mistake anywhere. My Inner Voice was right when it said, "Don't touch it," for I would have messed up things had I touched it then. And the Voice was right again when it said, "Now is the time to get out." I could not have resigned at any other moment during the day.

But why should the whole episode have happened at all? I can see as I look back across the years that those twenty-four hours were a deep purging of my spirit from any remnants of inward questionings and conflicts over my life work. All alternatives to being an evangelist were burned out in the fires of that day. If I could not leave being an evangelist to be a bishop, could I leave it for anything else? Hardly. I have gone through all the honors of being a bishop, have tasted the glory of it, and now know that for me there is no honor save being an evangelist, the bearer of Good News.

And perhaps the Church too made no mistake in its voting, for as a result of it all there came the thought to many an obscure minister, who would never gain position in the Church: "Well, I too am a bearer of the Good News. I do not need any position added to that. Let that suffice me." And perhaps he stood a little straighter. At least, that is what I am told did happen.

And now when I am tempted by my sins to divide my loyalty, it is easier to say: "How can I? I won that great battle there, how dare I lose this smaller one? I am an evangelist. I cannot unfit myself to be *that.*"

And was I glad to find that when my wife received the second cable saying that I had resigned she "hit the ceiling," as she describes it? We were both satisfied that my place was the Indian Road, and as an evangelist on that Road.

"Why is he so happy?" asked a Hindu fellow pilgrim on the Indian Road. "What diet does he take?" I'll tell you why I am so happy, and what diet I take: "I'm happy because I'm on the Indian Road and happier because I bear Good News within my heart, and cannot help but speak of what I've seen and heard—I'm an evangelist. My diet is the will of God—when I feed on that I live. That's why I'm so happy."

CHAPTER X

WHAT DOES CHRISTIANITY DO FOR YOU?

The night before I was to leave the Indian Road for a Mission to the universities of the West, I was in a meeting in which Doctor Ambedkar, the outstanding leader of the outcastes of India, was present. They asked him to address this group of Christian workers. He replied in these words: "As you know, we of the Depressed Classes have not made our choice of any faith. We are in the negative stage of breaking with the old. I, therefore, have no word to say to you. But it seems to me, if I may say so, that the more befitting thing, under the circumstances, would be for you to tell me what Christianity does for you. Just what does it do for you?"

We felt at once an electric interest seize the situation. Here we were face to face with a challenge that went straight to the center of things. For Doctor Ambedkar really represented two distinct groups. First, he represented the very modern man, highly educated and thoughtful, but without a vital faith. The old was dead, the new not yet born. The house of Man Soul was, like the New Testament figure, swept, garnished and empty. It was swept of old superstitions, garnished with many facts and conveniences of science, but empty of a positive, transforming faith. If he represented the modern man, that was challenge enough. But, second, he represented, as it were, the sixty million outcastes of India. He had assumed leadership among when before ten thousand outcastes he announced that while he was born a Hindu, he would not die one, that he was leaving Hinduism with as many of the outcastes as would follow him. What faith they would choose was yet to be decided. They would weigh the relative merits of the different faiths and make their choice.

Of course such a movement would be shot through and through with all sorts of motives: political, economic, social, moral, and spiritual. But the one motive that gathered all lesser motives within itself was the motive to *rise*. Who can lightly discount such a motive? If any people on earth have earned the right to that motive, the patient outcastes of India through centuries of degradation have earned that right. It ill becomes people who stand on unearned social, economic, and political privileges disdainfully to talk about the movement being only a movement for social and political betterment. If that were all, even so, I should welcome it and thank God that the dead souls of men were at last awakening. But it is more than that. It is the rise of the inner life manifesting itself in outer demand. The outcaste prostitutes of Bombay sent representatives to Doctor Ambedkar saying: "We hear that the Depressed Classes are rising. We want to give up this life of ours. Will you help us into a more decent way to earn a living?" Here was a moral and spiritual element too. The fact is that this whole Depressed Classes' demand for opportunity and a full life is a matrix in which the seeds of the Kingdom of God may be sown.

At first it was thought that if these millions go to another faith, the political situation would be affected—they would carry with them the proportionate representation in the Legislative Assemblies. It would therefore throw the balance of political power in the country. But an examination of the Reform Scheme shows that there is no provision for change of representation by change of numbers. The Scheme as it now stands does not envisage any large-scale change in numbers in any religious community. If, therefore, the sixty million outcastes went over to another community, it would not change the political complexion.

Of course the Act could be amended to meet such a condition, but as it now stands, political power is not involved in change of faith. This is to the good for us as Christians, for we do not want political power through conversion. It simplifies the situation to have the political element in abeyance or eliminated. But it makes it more difficult for the Depressed Classes to move to another faith, for they carry no political privileges with them; in fact, they may lose what they have. This is no small disability. The Depressed Class leaders know this and yet they want change. Why? To me it seems to be the working of the very Spirit of God.

When, therefore, Doctor Ambedkar looked into the eyes of that group and asked, "What does Christianity do for you?" it was both the modern intellectual and the inarticulate millions of Depressed Classes asking for a faith to live by.

I do not know when a more penetrating challenge had ever been given to the Christian faith and one more far-reaching in its results. Did we have something that at one and the same time could meet the needs of the hard-hit modern scientific mind and the needs of this depressed mass of humanity struggling toward freedom?

The silence that followed the question was breathless. A pastor arose and said, "Christ gives me peace." Christ gives me peace—it was good, but not good enough. Peace —yes, but life needs more than peace. The answer, I am afraid, was typical. The pastor, accustomed to think in terms of life as individual and inward, gave too small an answer. It wasn't big enough to fit the total need, and that is what the situation demanded.

Just what does Christianity do for me? If by Christianity we mean the system of creed and practice built up around Christ through the centuries, then I must say, it sometimes thrills me, sometimes puzzles me and sometimes disgusts me. It sometimes thrills me, for I see that out of this system has come the world's best life, the world's best service, and the world's best hope. But it sometimes puzzles me, for I see that its answers often fall short of human need. And it sometimes disgusts me when I see that in the name of Christianity we have been small and cantankerous, sometimes vindictive and cruel, and sometimes we have warred. Yesterday I picked up a non-Christian daily paper with the news item from Spain telling of celebrating "the Christian victory by a religious procession and a full-dress bullfight." I shuddered, and I shudder more deeply as I see that we have gone to war again to save our faith from the vandalism of dictators. We shall save our faith from vandals, by being more beneficently strong than vandals!

Yes, Christianity sometimes disgusts me, sometimes puzzles me, and sometimes thrills me—all three, and yet the last grips me and holds me more than the other two. And I'll tell you why.

I see that the system built up around Christ is the garment He wears, but life, as He said, is more than raiment. He has to wear this system as He wore the mock scarlet robes at the Judgment Hall—and what a trial it must be to Him!—but through the incongruous robes men see the Person, and are compelled to cry, like Pilate, "Behold the Man!"

The first thing, then, that Christianity does is to present me with this Man. The fact is that this Man is Christianity, real Christianity. I am compelled to take only as much in this system built up around Him as is congruous with His mind and spirit. When, therefore, I am tempted as Peter was to get my eyes off Him and ask in bewilderment, "Lord, and what shall this man do?" I hear Him reply, "What is that to thee? follow thou Me." The issue is clear: I must follow no man and no system except as they follow Christ. Even in Scripture I follow what fits into His mind, and what does not, I feel no obligation to follow, for did He not say, "Ye have heard it said of old time, . . . but I say unto you"? He made Himself final even in Scripture.

Here, then, the issue is the Man. I am glad the issue is a Man instead of a system of ideas or a creed. For how can I understand life except through a life that becomes the Life? How can I understand the meaning of Goodness unless I see it operative in the storm and stress of life? How can I understand Beauty unless I see its form against the background of human ugliness? How can I see the meaning of Truth unless truth stands Incarnate?

As I talked with Dr. Hu Shih, the father of the Renaissance movement in China and an agnostic, he held my hand in both of his at the close of our talk and said, rather wistfully, "Yes, after all, you have a very great advantage in that your ideas are embodied in a Person." He saw that good ideas are powerless to regenerate a people unless those ideas are embodied. If good maxims could save a people, China would be the most saved nation in the world, for whole streets of China are filled with banners with good mottoes on them. But they have no power to regenerate. For the Word has never become flesh. Only when it does become flesh, does it shake us like a passion and make us new.

And what did this Man do among us? He met our temptations, minus our falls. He faced our sins, and yet never once was there a prayer for forgiveness upon His lips or a tear of penitence upon His cheek. He preached repentance to men, but Himself never repented. He urged men to turn, but He, Himself, never retraced a step that He ever took. He induced in men and women sorrow for sin, and yet He Himself never once said, "I too am sorry." He said when ye pray say, "Our Father . . . forgive us our trespasses," but He, Himself, never prayed that prayer. He said, "If ye then being evil," but He left Himself out of it. At the end He dispensed forgiveness to a dying thief, but He, Himself, never asked for it—never!

Here I stand in the presence of sheer miracle—the miracle of being, a moral miracle. Grant that central Miracle and the lesser miracles become credible in the light of this central Miracle. I do not believe in Jesus because of the miracles. I believe in the miracles because of Jesus. The question is not, Do such things as miracles happen? Rather the questions are: Would such things happen around Jesus? Being what He was, would He not do what He did? Being a miracle, would He not perform miracles? When I look into His eyes, I know He would open blind eyes. When I look into His face, I know that He would wipe the falling tears from the faces of stricken parents by raising their dead. When I look through His words and actions into His heart, I can read forgiveness there for the sinful. I tell you, anything can happen around a Man like this! Anything that is right. Yes, and this is more breath-taking—*everything* that is right. For I see here not only goodness, but goodness linked with power. The first impression Jesus made on John the Baptist was of might: "Who is mightier than I?" and the last impression He left on His disciples, in spite of their sorrow, was: "A man mighty in deed and word." And between those two statements the same impression was left on all who came in contact with Him: "A new teaching! With authority He commands even the unclean spirits and they obey Him." And Pilate, who was used to Roman might, "when he heard this, was the more afraid." Afraid of a Prisoner! With mingled fear and admiration Pilate cried, "Behold the Man!" and we, with adoration mingled with fear, still cry, "Behold the Man!" "Mingled with fear"? Yes, for this Man sets our consciences fluttering like an electric needle in a storm. For He has authority there—at the center of our moral being, the conscience. The conscience answers to this Man—and to nothing else. What matters it who holds other territory in life as long as one holds the citadel of the being, the conscience? The future of the world belongs to the One to whom conscience belongs. The conscience belongs to Christ and therefore the future of the world belongs to Him.

The first thing that Christianity gives to me is the Man! This Man becomes my starting point, from which I work out to all the problems of life. I work out from Him to God. I do not work from God down to Him to see whether Christ is Godlike. But I work out from Him to God to see whether God is Christlike. A Moslem friend objected and said that I should work from God to see if Christ was Godlike. But had I done so, I would have come out at the place where he came out: Allah, instead of where I came out: the God and Father of our Lord Jesus Christ. In one case, I would have come out to a despotic throne, and in the other case, I came out at a Cross. I do not regret my landing place. How can we work from God down since in doing so, I would have to posit the kind of God I begin with. Then my thought of God is the beginning place. So I do not begin with God, I begin with my own thought, with myself. I am the Revelation.

The man who says he can go straight to God without a medium forgets that we must all have a medium—our own thoughts and conceptions, other peoples' thoughts and conceptions, a Book—all these are mediums through which we go to God. I prefer this Person. For I know nothing higher for God or man than to be Christlike. I analyze the tiny sunbeam and can tell the constituent elements of the vast sun. I gaze upon the character of

Christ, and lo, I know the constituent elements of the universe, God. And the God I see is utterly, completely, overwhelmingly satisfying—and saving!

But I not only work from Christ to God, I work from Christ to man. I have difficulty in holding my faith in man when I see his stupidities and cruelties, building up civilization with one hand and tearing it down with the other through wars. Should we not acquiesce in the judgment of the modern cynic when he says that "man is only a parasitic louse on the body of a dying world"? I am afraid that is where I would have to come out with man were it not for this Man. But this Man holds me steady. For in Him I see not only what God is like, but what man can become like. If "He is the first-born of a great brotherhood" then there is dignity, meaning, and possibility in the Family. He, as the Elder Brother of a guilty Family, has borne the Family guilt. A man is no longer a man, he is "a man for whom Christ died." The blood marks are no longer sprinkled on the lintels of the door to save from the angel of death; they are now sprinkled on our foreheads to save us from the deadly pessimisms about man. As the Hindu wears his vermilion spot upon his brow to proclaim to the world that he belongs to his god, so every man, whether he wants to wear it or not, has the blood mark of the Son of God upon his brow. The mark of Cain may be there too, for both Cain, the murderer of his brother, and Christ, the Redeemer of His brothers, claim man, and the struggle goes on within the will of man as to which shall have his allegiance. That struggle is going on today on a world scale, and if man collectively decides to be Cain and proceeds to murder his brother, this time he does it with rationalizations upon his lips, arguing that he is doing it in the name of justice, and even for the sake of Christ. Man may argue, twist, explain away, but in his heart of hearts, he knows who has him. He knows he has been hooked by the love of Christ and must in the end belong to Him. Professor John MacMurray is right when he says that there is one issue and one issue alone in Europe today—Christianity. Down underneath all issues is that one issue. The Cain spirit and the Christ spirit are struggling for the mastery of the world today. But that very struggle is a sign of man's worthwhileness. There is something within him that won't let him go to hell easily. He may in the end decide that he cannot go to hell at all, not with this Mark on his brow. Westerners living in India argue that they have a stake in India through huge investments and must thereby help decide the future. Christ has a stake in the world—that stake is a cross, driven deep into the soul of humanity and that investment of a Divine life in human life tells me that in the end this Man will decide our destiny. I believe in man because I believe in this Man.

But it does more than give me faith in man, it gives me faith in this man, myself. When I cannot believe in myself, He makes me do so. My capacity to blunder drove me to His feet in the beginning, and it keeps me there. I came to Him not on an intellectual quest for intellectual peace, but for moral healing. The battle of my mind was great, the battle of my emotion was greater, but I knew the battle of my will was decisive. I had gone wrong there—at the center of my being, the place of my choices, my will. And He healed me there, righted me at the center, gave me what I most needed: forgiveness, reconciliation with God and myself. I say "myself," for I could not live with myself until this sense of wrongness was gone.

The modern man lashes at his circumstances and at other men because he is not at peace with himself. He needs nothing so much as he needs reconciliation with himself, and he knows he cannot be reconciled with himself until he is reconciled with this Christ who troubles him from within.

Henri Busse tells the story of the soldier dying at the front and saying to his comrade: "I'm done for. I am passing out. There are no marks on my card against me. You have lived an evil life and your card is badly marked. You take my card and with it my name and live by that name and card. I'm taking your card and it will be buried with me." Christ actually does that—and more. He took my card and died and buried it, and all that it stood for, in the grave with Himself. And then He asked me to take His card—His card without a mark on it as my own. And, more wonderful still, He asked me to take His name—Christ-ian—and live by it. I was to live in His stead, representing Him.

What a dignity has come within my bosom! I live representing Him, entrusted with His card. That fact stands between me and my old life. How dare I besmirch His card and dishonor His name? That is the moral position His redemption landed me in. I took a gift and found an obligation, a constraint. I took a liberty and it turned into a law operative at the very center of my moral consciousness. I was free from the old life, but utterly bound to the new life. There was an exchange of selves: He took mine and I took His. "I am crucified with Christ: nevertheless I live; yet not I, but Christ liveth in me: and the life which I now live ... I live by the faith of the Son of God." Christianity does that for me.

But it does something else for me. It not only gives me the right to forgive myself, but it gives me the power to forgive others. Seeley says forgiveness of injuries is the central Christian virtue. How impossible a thing it seems—until you see Him! Then how impossible to do anything else and stay in His company! This impulse

comes to the simplest followers. In South India a village
man became a Christian. It aroused his caste people
against him to bitter enmity. They came and stole his
harvest, reaping it at night. He came upon them while
they were in the act, fell down before them beseeching
them with folded hands to leave some of the precious grain
for the sustenance of his family. They cut off both his
hands as he folded them beseechingly before them. That
was their answer. And what would his be? His enemies waited the summons to court to answer the charge.
Many counseled him to prosecute them. He refused.
Christ had forgiven him, he would forgive them for
Christ's sake. So astonished were his enemies at this
offensive of love and so inwardly changed were they at
this treatment that they restored the grain, and in an attempt at atonement plowed and sowed and reaped his
fields and did his work for him, since he was handless and
helpless. Helpless? By that spirit He has helped us all
to see into the very heart of the Christian faith. Handless?
By that same spirit he reaches out a helping hand to
those of us who are sinking into the waves of resentment
and hate.

When the anti-Christian movement swept across China
and struck Nanking, a missionary friend of mine determined that he would try the Sermon on the Mount as his
way of meeting the crisis. When the crowd broke into
his compound, a soldier struck him with the butt of his
gun on one side of his chest and he offered the other to
be smitten. The soldier looked at him in helpless surprise. He went into his house and found the people loot-
ing everything. A well-dressed man was trying alone to
get his brass bed down the steps, but it got caught. My
friend took hold of the other end of the bed and said, "Let
me help you." The Chinese blushed to the roots of his
hair and fled out of the house. In the compound he found

them trying in vain to open his tins of fruit and vegetables. He asked them to bring them to him and he opened them for them. And when they asked what was inside the tins he told them. They took hold of him to lead him off to execute him. He put his arm through the arm of the ringleader and said: "You are my protector. I am depending on you to be my protector and friend." So he marched arm in arm with his chief executioner. But as they went along the atmosphere changed at his astonishing good will. The procession stopped, and so bursting with good will did the atmosphere become that they decided to send him back free, but before he went they actually raised a cheer, "Three cheers for America." He had conquered—as a Christian!

Some day we will learn that method as our collective way of life, and when we do, we will make more advance in a decade than we have done in centuries. Now we match hate with hate, armament with armament, force with force, and Satan tries to cast out Satan.

Christianity gives one power to forgive injuries, not because we are not strong enough to resist, but we are so strong we can resist from a higher level. The enemy strikes you on one cheek and you strike him on the heart by turning the other cheek. You wrest the offensive from him by your daring offensive of love. A man gave me the greatest insult possible from one human to another. I seized him by his thin neck with both my hands and said, "I've got power to close my hands and choke you to death, but I forgive you." I woke and found it was a dream, but in my heart I knew that whether waking or sleeping, this was the way to treat an enemy: Forgive him, not because you are so weak you can do nothing else, but because you are so strong you can restrain yourself and assume the offensive of love.

But not only does Christianity give one power to forgive

injuries, it also gives power to face adverse circumstances, injustices, and unmerited suffering. This dark problem of unmerited suffering lights up as we see what happened at the cross. Jesus did not bear the cross—He used it. The cross was sin, and He turned it into the healing of sin; the cross was hate, and He turned it into a manifestation of the love of God. The cross showed man at his worst, and there Jesus shows God at His redemptive best. The cruelest, darkest word that life ever spoke was at the cross, and Jesus took all that cruelty and darkness and turned it into pure love and pure light. Jesus took hold of everything that ever spoke against the love of God and through those very things showed the love of God. What a light it sheds upon the tragedy of life to have such a fact at the center of our faith! Without the cross, the righteous are compelled to expect exemption from suffering as the ancient Hebrews did, or an exact requital for all deeds as the Hindus do, or to meekly submit to suffering as the will of God as the Moslems do, or to steel oneself against the sufferings of life as the Stoics did—"my head might be bloody, but it will be unbowed under the bludgeonings of chance." The last named is good, but not good enough. The Christian goes beyond that, and all the rest of the ways we have mentioned, for he not only bears suffering, he uses it. He lays hold on the raw materials of human living, pleasure and pain, compliment and criticism, justice and injustice, and takes them up into the purpose of his life as the lotus takes the muck and mire and transforms it into the beauty of the lotus flower. A bomb smashed the side of a mission bungalow in China and they took the debris and out of it built a chapel. I mean the moral and spiritual equivalent of that—taking hold of the debris of life when life falls into ruins around one and making out of it something more beautiful—a chapel. Newton was forced to leave his studies at Cambridge at twenty-three on account of plague, and during the period of eighteen months of enforced vacation he discovered differential calculus, the composition of light, and the law of gravitation! Driven out by plague into that achievement! In Australia I came in contact with a woman who met a supreme tragedy in a supreme way. Both of her arms and both of her legs were cut off, the arms near the shoulders and the legs near the hips, leaving only a stump of a person. Only a stump of a person? By no means, for she gathered up the remnants of life and made them into a beautiful shrine for the indwelling of God. She invented a contraption to fasten on her arm and she writes a beautiful letter with it, one of which I have as my prized possession. She has written a book entitled *Sunshine and Shadows,* the story of how she met life. People sit around her bed to learn from her how to live. Christ is taking that stump of a life and transforming it into an instrument of God. L. P. Jacks is right when he says: "The man whom the gods love is the man who stands up to the challenge of life. If you 'withstand' him like a man, your enemy proves himself 'beautiful'; he becomes your friend at need; is found at your side at the moment when all seems lost; his strength made perfect in your weakness; his shield thrown round you; his right arm bare in your defense. . . . But if you fall to complaining and self-pity; if you go after your own ease and happiness; if you hire a substitute to carry your load, the beauty of your enemy will never be seen by you." Christ gives you power to make your very enemies subserve your ends. He offers us a positive, active way of dealing with suffering, and this method, says James, "gives a new dimension to life."

But not only does Christianity give power to stand up against life, it also gives power to be interested in life, even unlovable life—it teaches us to care, makes us sensitive to human need. "It's not on my shoulders," not my responsibility, is a common Chinese saying. And that is the usual attitude of the human heart until Christ comes, and then we really learn to care, we are sensitized. The process of Christianizing is the process of sensitizing. With all the stupidities and follies of missionary endeavor, yet it spells out one thing: they really care how men live, how all men live. I know a missionary who would sit up all night with his sweeper Christians, down among the latrines where they lived, to keep them from drinking during their wedding festivities—because he cared. I know another who on furlough said concerning her outcaste children, "I can't sleep nights for thinking about them," because she cared. A high-caste Christian boy gave his blood for a blood transfusion to a Mohammedan youth, because he cared. Doctor Summerville came within eight hundred feet of the top of Everest and gained fame and name, but he then proceeded to bury himself in an obscure town in Travancore and now operates on stricken bodies often till past midnight till he is almost ready to drop from exhaustion, because he cares. Some cultured and able Maoris came over to Australia from New Zealand to celebrate the anniversary of the sending of missionaries to them. As they returned, two of the ablest, a man and his wife, volunteered to come back to the Aboriginals of Australia, as missionaries, because they cared. In the Fiji Islands I stood on a platform underneath which were buried the bones of a missionary who had been killed and eaten by the cannibals. The sons and daughters of those cannibals were in front of me, and they were cultured and refined and so musical they could break into Handel's "Hallelujah Chorus," in parts, without a leader, and do it exquisitely. A missionary told me how he had tried to get their fathers to give up their cannibalism by holding up a skull to them and saying: "This is the skull of your brother. And you have eaten him."

They burst into laughter and replied, "It's not the skull of our brother; it's the skull of a pig"—a pig because he belonged to another tribe. Their brotherhood did not go beyond their tribe. But after they became Christians, they heard there was famine in India, and they took a large collection to send to save the famine-stricken. They had come in contact with Christ, and now they were so sensitized that their brotherhood extended beyond their tribe to people whom they had never seen, thousands of miles across the seas. Now they cared. "Caring is the biggest thing out," Van Hugel said, "Christianity taught us to care." It did. Long before anyone else cared for the outcastes of India, the Christians cared. It's only the Christians who have schools for the blind and the dumb, and asylums for lepers.

In the onward march of life, the oyster did a fatal thing: it put its nervous system on the inside and put its skeleton on the outside—it would protect itself from pain and suffering. The beings to which we belong did a dangerous thing: they put their skeletons on the inside and their nervous system on the outside. They would be sensitive to surrounding life and would suffer. They did—and rose! The oyster fastened itself upon a rock, refused to suffer—and stayed where it was as life swept on past it. The future belongs to the sensitized. If so, it really belongs to the Christian, for the Christian cares more than any man I know. The Begum of ——, an enlightened Moslem ruler, had a dream that she was very thirsty, and as she expressed her desire for a drink, Mohammed turned his back, but Christ gave her a drink. She awoke troubled and called her learned ulemas and maulvis to interpret the dream. They reported that it meant that Her Highness was to dismiss all the Christians from the State service. "I will," replied Her Highness, "provided you can get me people just as honest and people who care as much as these Christians do." Christ does make us care. And some day we shall care without distinction of birth and class and color, and shall not rest until the last and least have shared with us all our privileges. We cannot be oysters again, clamped within our shell, sensitive only to our own desires, for Christ's love has dissolved our shell and has exposed us to all the world and its need. We do care, and we cannot help it. Christianity does that for us.

But I hear the murmured objection: It is all very well, and we are impressed, but all you say is individual and leaves untouched the great social and economic problems. What does Christianity do for you there?

It gives me the Kingdom of God, a totalitarian Order more totalitarian than any of those now proposed, an Order which includes within itself all life, individual and social. I really should have begun with the Kingdom of God, for there is where Christ began. He threw around all His teaching concerning the personal this all-embracing Order, and everything He said must be seen in the light of that framework. If we miss that framework, we miss the significance of His teaching. A noted economist, Sir Josiah Stamp, put his microscope to the teachings of Jesus in his book, *Christianity and Economics,* to see what He taught on economics, and came to the conclusion that He taught very little, so that His teachings give little direction on such problems—they must be looked on as giving directions and dynamic for personal life alone, and only incidentally on social and economic questions. Apart from the fact that the author himself is deeply embedded in this old order and would be very greatly disturbed if it were disturbed, why was it that he missed the social and economic significance of the teachings and life of Jesus? For the simple reason that he almost entirely ignored the framework of the teaching of Jesus—the Kingdom of God. He scarcely mentioned it, and yet Jesus used it more than He used any other single thing. It is like discussing England and leaving out of your thinking the British Empire, the framework in which England lives and moves and has her being. If you leave out the Kingdom of God, you miss the master-conception which held within itself all relationships of God and man and material in an all-embracing Kingdom in which everything finds purpose, meaning, integration, and goal. If God rules at all, He must rule over the whole of life; there must be no half-God ruling over a half-realm. No teaching about economics and social living? The whole groundwork, framework, and atmosphere are nothing but the individual relating himself to the totality of life and the totality of life relating itself to the individual. Life is one; in the Kingdom all compartmentalisms go down, life must be dealt with as a whole. I must bring material things and social relations under one reign—the law of love. If I do, then life is bound to shift its basis from this ruthlessly competitive order to a cooperative order. Moreover, if I make love the law of life, then I must treat every man as a brother apart from the question of race, or birth, or class, or color. "One is your Father, and all ye are brethren."

So, amid all the changing back and forth in trial and error of this way and that way of life, I know that we must come at last to God's way—the Kingdom of God. For this is the Kingdom built from the foundation of the world, and built within the foundation of the world, so the world and all it contains will work no other way.

Did Christianity not give me this conception as the background of all my thinking I would be utterly at sea in this time of social and economic and individual flux. But with it I hold steady, for we shall run up the roads of Fascism, Communism, and capitalism, and find they are roads with dead ends, but one day we shall try the Kingdom of God. And then we shall be like a railway train off the rails, bumping along the ties, tearing itself and its tracks to pieces, when suddenly it finds the rails again and now harmoniously and rhythmically it goes its way to its destination.

Christianity gives me a master-conception and thus gathers all of life's meanings into a central whole. I have my answer ready when a chastened world wants to know the Way—this is the Way, for it is God's way. I can afford to wait, for I know the answer will be sought.

But Christianity does something else for me. It teaches me that the Kingdom is not only going to function in this world, but in the world to come. "May Thy Kingdom come, may Thy will be done on earth as it is done in heaven." The Kingdom is now completely functioning and that functioning is heaven. I enter now a Kingdom which has eternal meaning. The moment I enter it I know that this is an unshakable Kingdom, unshakable by the shock of death. All other kingdoms are shakable—have we not seen the processions of the kingdoms through history on their way to the dust? This one has survival value, it fits the facts, it is founded on the very pillars on which the universe is founded. I shall, therefore, not be afraid of death. For this Kingdom, personalized in Christ, was crucified, and buried by the supreme kingdom of this world, Rome, and lo! it arose again from the dead. I thus belong to a deathless Kingdom, and shall not be afraid of death. Should the chrysalis be afraid of the rending of its bonds, when those broken bonds mean a butterfly? Should the foul earth be afraid of losing its moorings when taken hold of by the roots of the lotus, when that losing shall be the finding of the beauty of the lotus flower? Should the seed shudder with horror as it bursts its shell through swelling life, when that bursting means the bloom? Nor shall I be afraid when death snaps my bonds, for it is only a snapping of the bonds and not a snapping of the central thing at the core of my being—the Kingdom of God. That is unshakable.

One of the devoted members of our Ashram faced death, stricken with a cancer at the very prime of her life when she was so fitted to battle with mass-illiteracy. As death approached she wrote me these words, "The road leads uphill all the way, but the scenery is getting grander and grander. I am worshiping Christ just now in the beauty of the sweetpeas. Yours in the Glad Service of Waiting." And again: "The house that Grace Chapman lives in is tumbling to pieces, but as the cracks get wider and wider I trust that the love of Christ within me can shine through all the better." It did shine through all the better. The doctor reverently said, "It's sheer miracle—she is living off pure spirit." To that pure spirit death was unbelievably unreal. This was the reality—the Kingdom within her. No wonder Jesus said that the Kingdom and Life were synonymous. They are, and she, having that Kingdom, had that Life—deathless Life.

Christianity, then, does this for me—it gives me an unshakable faith that life survives the dissolution of its wrappings. Do not discuss with me the doctrine of immortality. I am not discussing bare immortality apart from this Kingdom. Whether men survive apart from this Kingdom I do not know. But that they do survive in this Kingdom I am assured. It has the feel of the real and the eternal upon it. It fits the facts.

Christianity does another thing for me—it gives me an inner steadiness. I am held together at the center. One of the most striking passages out of early Christian literature is in the Epistle of Diognetus: "What the soul is to the body the Christians are to the world. They hold the world together." The Christians hold the world together! This was written at the time when the old order was decaying around them—the Roman Empire was in the state of dissolution. Amid that going to pieces, the writer saw that there was a people who were not going to pieces. They held steady as partaking of an unshockable Kingdom. The Christians held the world together then, they must and will hold the world together now. For we are in the midst of a similar period of decay. The old order is going to pieces around us. Men's hearts are fainting with fear at the things which are about to come upon the earth. Jesus added this word, "You will hear of wars and rumors of wars: see and be not afraid." The absence of fear was not because they refused to look at the facts—they were bidden, "See, and be not afraid." They were to see things, to be realistic, not try to have peace by refusal to look at the facts. They were to look at the worst and be unafraid. Why? Because, being inwardly held together, they were to hold the world together.

The Christians again will have to hold the world together. They can do so because they have a center for life—God; they are immovably fixed in Him. You cannot hold the world together on atheism, for if you lose God, you lose the meaning of life, the bottom drops out of things, your universe turns dead upon your hands. No wonder Christianity has been called "cosmic optimism." It believes that the worst can become the best, that the weak can become strong, the defeated victorious.

The Christians will hold the world together because their Kingdom demands equal treatment for all apart from extraneous things such as race and birth and class and money. You cannot hold the world together on the basis of unequal treatment. That is being tried now, and the world has toppled over into war and revolution. The dispossessed soon become the disease in any society. The Christians cannot tolerate any dispossessed.

The Christians hold the world together because their Kingdom offers justice as the basis of relationships—justice, not charity, or vague good will. "The Kingdom of God is righteousness, peace, and joy in the Holy Ghost" —note that righteousness, just human relationships, comes before peace. We do not expect peace without a fundamental justice at the basis of human society. You cannot hold the world together on the basis of injustice, even though that injustice be backed by military might, for the injustice will finally break your sword and destroy your might. The only thing that will hold the world together is justice.

The Christians hold the world together for another reason: they make love their motive and driving force. After hate has done its destructive work, love must gather up the fragments and construct things again. Hate cannot do that. Shells can blow things to pieces, but cannot put them together again. They have no germ of life within them. Love has the seed of life within itself, so it will outlast all force and all hate.

Again the Christians hold the world together, for they do not know when they are defeated. With a faith founded on a supreme Defeat, the Cross, which became the world's supreme Victory, how can they be defeated by lesser defeats? They live by defeat—they lose their life centrally and fundamentally, and having surrendered there, where else shall they surrender? Having consented to die at the central place of the self, what can death now do to them? If a pessimist is a man who sees a difficulty in an opportunity, a Christian is one who sees an opportunity in a difficulty. He sees an Easter morning in every Calvary, a sunrise in every midnight. They have seen the worst and believe in the best. They have descended into hell, only to open its gates to release its prisoners.

Chang Poling was the most discouraged man in China —he saw his country sinking into ruin, and Confucian ethics were powerless to regenerate the land. So discouraged did he become that he suggested to some of his friends that they form a Suicide Pact, in which they would all commit suicide to shock the country into doing something. It was a counsel of despair. But he got hold of a New Testament before committing suicide, and it threw a flood of light into his darkness—here was good teaching and power in one; here were weak men becoming strong and discouraged men becoming radiant. He became a Christian—he would not die for China, he would live for China. He set up the great Nankai University at Tientsin, and when it was deliberately destroyed by Japanese bombs, he moved two thousand miles back into the interior at Chungking and set up another school. His son killed as an aviator over Shanghai, his university destroyed, he starts all over again—unbeatable!

The Christians hold the world together because they have a conception bigger than the world—the Kingdom of God. Why should I feel the universe has gone to pieces with a disturbance upon this midget planet of ours, when God rules in the furtherest star and in the tiniest atom? If there is convulsion on my world, I know it is God sending the eagles where decay is found. He is breaking up this old order to give us a new one. The nemesis has come that the new might emerge. The Kingdom of God holds me steady when the demand for economic and social change becomes insistent. I have my new foundation ready to put under the old.

I shall not be too disturbed at the tread of dictators. I know they can cause a terrible amount of destruction. But they have their day and cease to be. In coming out to India by plane, we left Marseilles in the early morning and stopped for fueling at Corsica, from which island

Napoleon went forth to conquer a world. At noon we lunched at Naples, the land from which the Caesars went to subdue the earth. At nightfall we were in Corfu, Greece, from which land Alexander went to be a world conqueror. On another hop we flew past Assyria on the right, and on the left, Babylon, from which the mighty kings went forth to make the earth tremble; and then over Persia from which land Darius and others went to make the earth into vassal states—twenty-four in their list, so the figures on the ruins say. The next day we were in Karachi, the land of Ind, over which the mighty Mogul conquerors held their sway.

But as I looked down for two days over the empires going out from beneath me, I was struck with the fact that every one of those mighty empires with their dread dictators are dead and gone. Napoleon lasted for twenty years and had his Saint Helena; Caesar had his Brutus; Alexander died in a drunken brawl in Babylon, trying to conquer a world and unable to conquer himself; Babylon is a ruin that only the experts can decipher; the Persian conquerors are inscribed only in crumbling ruins; and the Moghul conquerors exist only in a few splendid monuments—their empires are dead and gone. They were broken on the fact of God. Their evils were their undoing.

Will modern empires and States founded on blood and fear last while those others did not? Hardly. They too will break themselves on God. "For every plant which my heavenly Father hath not planted shall be rooted up"—that verse spells the death knell of all oppression and aggression. But Thy Kingdom, O God, is an everlasting Kingdom. It will outlast and outwear all the kingdoms founded on selfishness and fear and blood. And the rule of Mammon will go down as did the rule of the Sword—plutocracy and autocracy will alike crumble before the onmarch of God. You cannot stop God and you cannot stop Man. Hinder them? Yes, but you cannot stop them.

The Christians hold the world together because they look beyond these kingdoms which bluster and strut and rattle their swords to a Kingdom founded on the imponderables of justice and love—a cross, and they are held steady amid the flux of daily happenings. I failed to mention that our aeroplane, in going over the ruins of these mighty empires, went past a hill called Calvary where a Man went forth to die to found a Kingdom on love. The land in which He did it was so obscure and the hill so low, and the Man so lacking in kingly splendor, that one might easily pass it by. And yet—and yet that Kingdom of love which He founded that day will outwear those other Kingdoms. When the years and the centuries have spoken against the hours, they will proclaim the fitness of this Man to rule—and no other.

But the Christians hold the world together for another reason—they, themselves, are inwardly held together by an inward constraint—the love of Christ. Those who submit to Him undergo the change of their master-sentiment and life is unified around a central allegiance. Held together at the center of life they do not fly to pieces at the circumference.

When Paul tried to express this wonderful power of Christ to hold things together, he said, "In him all things consist," or hold together. They do. In everything else a centrifugal force that makes men and situations fly apart is at work. In Him, all things hold together, for He is love, and love binds together. Hate, selfishness, greed, lust, envy—all these drive men apart, and hence have the seeds of their own destruction within them. Only in Christ do all things hold together.

So in answer to Doctor Ambedkar, the modern man and

the leader of aspiring outcastes, when he asks, "What does Christianity do for you?" I can say, "Well, *everything!* It does not solve all my questions in neat, ready-made answers, but it gives me a Key, a Master Key to unlock each situation and each problem as it comes.

Do not tell me that my Key is too simple for the growing complexities and intricacies of modern life, and is out-moded and outgrown. My objector may have that fear, because he has not this Fact. I have no such fear, for I see Him not only behind me in history, but beside me and beyond me. And do not fear that we rest in a static man-ner upon a static past. Christ breaks up all my compla-cencies. He rests me and never lets me rest. He gives me peace and then sends me out to battle. He gives me security and then breaks it up with a new adventure. I can understand what Paul meant when he said, "By all the stimulus of Christ"—stimulus is the word. An in-ward goad that drives you on and on. But it is not merely a stimulus of the soul, but a stimulus of the whole being —body, mind, and spirit. All need of stimulants for the body drop away—we have one. All need for excitements for jaded minds are unnecessary, we have a supreme ex-citement, the bringing in of a new Order on earth. All necessity for pick-me-ups for discouraged and fearful souls is gone, for we have an inward stimulus of love that drives out all fear and discouragement and defeatism. And, more than this, we have the words of our Master saying that social molds would also be broken up under the expansive pressure of the new wine of the Kingdom. We therefore feel that God is on the side of the fermenting wine, more than He is on the side of the retaining wine-skins. He is in the spirit of divine discontent throughout the world as well as in the forces of law and order. We are, therefore, no worshipers of the great god Is, but we do bow at the shrine of the Ought-to-be. Christ is in the past giving us the supreme Norm, in the present giving us a supreme release and power, and in the future giving us the supreme adventure. If Christ is not the answer—then there is no answer.

So, as we journey along the Indian Road, we face the future with confidence, even with a song. For, if the future of India demands a new order—and it is right now demanding a new social and economic order—we have a new Order to offer—the Kingdom of God. If that future demands new character to undergird and uphold these changes, then we know in Christ we have a power that makes new character out of old. If that future demands an undiscouraged dynamic to keep men going when discouragements assail, then we have, in Christ, a dynamic to keep men going, for our gospel is a gospel of "in spite of," a gospel that has scars on it, but radiant scars, a gospel that knows no turning back. And if India needs assurance of something not outgrowable as she lets go an outgrown past, then I know we have in Christ something that cannot be outgrown—Life itself. Can you outgrow Life?

Do not tell me that the Church is divided and weak and often trivial. I know that. I feel it to the depths of my being. Have I not been up against that fact for thirty-two years? And yet that divided, weak, and often trivial Church has within it the germs of a new life. We know "we have this treasure in earthen vessels," but then we do have this treasure, however earthen the vessel may be. And we must not be so obsessed with the earthenness of the vessel and forget the treasure, Christ. I came away from hauling over the coals a Christian congregation, for being so unchristian, for being so weak and unaggressive. As I went away from the church I came across a procession going along the road in which devotees were prostrating themselves in the dust before the goddess of smallpox.

My reaction was immediate: Those people I have been censuring have come from this—this that I have seen in this procession. They are now cultured and refined and educated, and more than that—with all their faults they have within them the germs of a new life. And more: they are part of a world fellowship stretching across race and class—a world brotherhood of the Christian Church. This procession has no such germ—it belongs to a dying superstitious past. It had no such world fellowship. Never again will I blame that congregation as I did this morning. For if I must call attention to their sins, it will be with an undertone of faith and hope, for the Dynamic is at work in their midst in spite of everything. That this Dynamic is at work, I see from the fact that in three of the sacred cities of India when the municipalities became so corrupt that they had to be superseded by Government, three Christians were put in charge of them to straighten them out; at least one of whom had been an outcaste—an outcaste Christian head of a Brahmin city!

And do not tell me that we missionaries are often wooden, narrow, racial, and self-assertive. I know that too—all too well. There are no sins that we have not been guilty of. But in spite of it all, we know that we are presenting something bigger than ourselves. And something which, when all is said and done, does not depend upon ourselves. We have no right of eminent domain over the Kingdom of God. It may be that God will find better instruments of the Kingdom in the lands to which we go who may carry it on to completion within those lands and to the rest of the world, including the lands from which we missionaries come. That may all be true, and yet of one thing we are sure: If the human race is to be religious at all in the future, it must be religious according to the spirit of Jesus Christ, or not be religious at all. If it is going to worship any God at all, it must be a God like the Father of our Lord Jesus Christ. If it is going to want any all-embracing Kingdom which will save it from its own selfishnesses and consequent tensions, then it must be the Kingdom of God. If it is going to want a saviour from individual and collective sin, then there is no other on the field seriously bidding for the heart of the world except Jesus Christ, the Saviour. If the world wants a Cause—a supreme Cause and a person embodying that Cause—then that Cause is the Kingdom and that supreme Person embodying that Cause is Christ.

"I suppose after all," said John Dewey, the Humanist, on one occasion during an educational visit to China, "that you missionaries have got hold of the right end of things." We have got hold of the right end of things, for that end is Christ.